SCIENTISTS AND THEIR DISCOVERIES
THOMAS EDISON

SCIENTISTS AND THEIR DISCOVERIES

ALBERT EINSTEIN

ALEXANDER FLEMING

ALFRED NOBEL

BENJAMIN FRANKLIN

CHARLES DARWIN

GALILEO

GREGOR MENDEL

ISAAC NEWTON

LEONARDO DA VINCI

LOUIS PASTEUR

THOMAS EDISON

SCIENTISTS AND THEIR DISCOVERIES
THOMAS EDISON

KAREN ELLIS

MASON CREST

Mason Crest
450 Parkway Drive, Suite D
Broomall, Pennsylvania 19008
(866) MCP-BOOK (toll-free)
www.masoncrest.com

Printed and bound in the United States of America.

CPSIA Compliance Information: Batch #SG2018.
For further information, contact Mason Crest at 1-866-MCP-Book.

First printing
9 8 7 6 5 4 3 2 1

Library of Congress Cataloging-in-Publication Data

ISBN: 978-1-4222-4034-2 (hc)
ISBN: 978-1-4222-7766-9 (ebook)

Scientists and their Discoveries series ISBN: 978-1-4222-4023-6

Developed and Produced by National Highlights Inc.
Interior and cover design: Yolanda Van Cooten
Production: Michelle Luke

CONTENTS

CHAPTER 1   The Young Inventor 7

CHAPTER 2   The Robber Barons 21

CHAPTER 3   The Wizard of Menlo Park 33

CHAPTER 4   Let There Be Light 45

CHAPTER 5   Losing Touch 59

CHAPTER 6   Recorded Music and Movies 69

                 Chronology 84

                 Further Reading 88

                 Internet Resources 89

                 Series Glossary of Key Terms 90

                 Index 92

                 About the Author 96

KEY ICONS TO LOOK FOR:

Words to understand: These words with their easy-to-understand definitions will increase the reader's understanding of the text while building vocabulary skills.

Sidebars: This boxed material within the main text allows readers to build knowledge, gain insights, explore possibilities, and broaden their perspectives by weaving together additional information to provide realistic and holistic perspectives.

Educational videos: Readers can view videos by scanning our QR codes, providing them with additional educational content to supplement the text. Examples include news coverage, moments in history, speeches, iconic sports moments, and much more!

Text-dependent questions: These questions send the reader back to the text for more careful attention to the evidence presented there.

Research projects: Readers are pointed toward areas of further inquiry connected to each chapter. Suggestions are provided for projects that encourage deeper research and analysis.

Series glossary of key terms: This back-of-the-book glossary contains terminology used throughout the series. Words found here increase the reader's ability to read and comprehend higher-level books and articles in this field.

Thomas Edison became very adept at sending messages on the Morse key, as this transmitter was called.

 WORDS TO UNDERSTAND

duplex—a telegraph circuit that can transmit two messages at once.

electromagnet—iron or steel magnetized by an electric current passing through a coil of wire surrounding it.

filibuster—unnecessarily long speech delivered to hold up business in an assembly.

Morse code—dot-and-dash system of representing the letters of the alphabet. Devised for telegraphists by U.S. inventor Samuel Morse (1791–1872).

patent—the exclusive right to make, use, or sell an invention for a given number of years.

telegraph—device for sending messages to a distant point by making and breaking an electric circuit in a connecting wire.

CHAPTER 1

The Young Inventor

Some men have the luck to live at exactly the right time. Thomas Alva Edison was one of them. In 1847, America was largely a farming country with a population of 20 million. By Edison's death in 1931, it had grown into the richest and most technologically advanced nation in the world with a population of 120 million. Edison's genius for invention helped to make that growth possible.

He was born on February 11, 1847, in Milan, Ohio. His father, Samuel Edison, was a tall, lean, jack-of-all-trades of Dutch stock. As a tavern keeper at Vienna in Ontario, Canada, he had married Nancy Elliott, a village schoolteacher. In 1837, he joined a rebellion against the Canadian government and, when it failed, fled across the border to America, settling in Milan, which at the time was a rapidly growing port on the Huron Canal. There he was joined by his wife and four children. He made a fair living as a lumber merchant.

In Milan, three more children were born. The youngest was Thomas Alva. He was an odd-looking boy with a large head, a round face, fair hair, and blue eyes. He was always asking questions and he would, whenever possible, test out the answers for himself. When told that geese hatched out their eggs by sitting on them, he made a nest in the barn, put some eggs in it, and sat on them for hours.

His father, Sam, thought him stupid. Both he and Mrs. Edison frequently whipped him with a birch switch, but Thomas still got into scrapes.

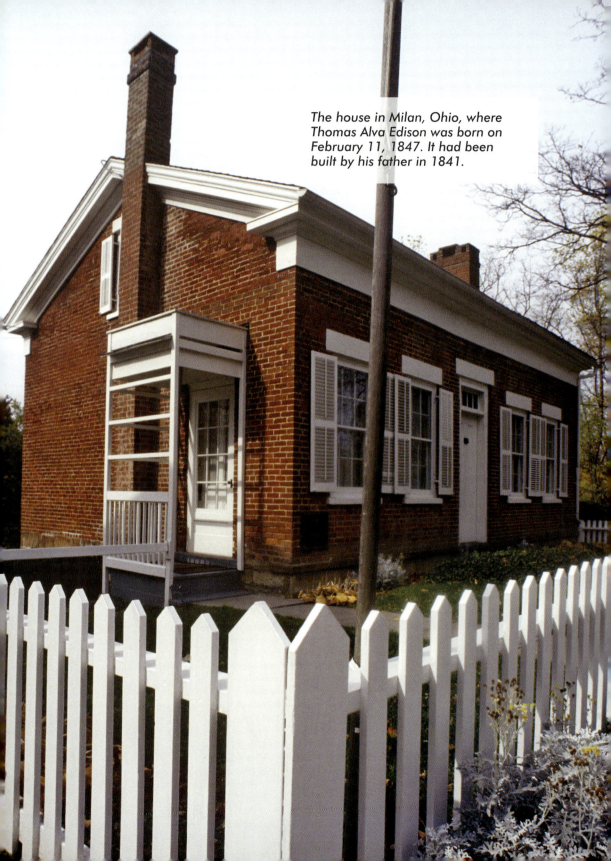

The house in Milan, Ohio, where Thomas Alva Edison was born on February 11, 1847. It had been built by his father in 1841.

Thomas's mother and father, Nancy Elliott Edison and Samuel Ogden Edison Jr.

Experimenting with fire one day, he burned down his father's barn. Sam Edison called out all his neighbors and their children and thrashed his six-year-old son in the village square.

Young Entrepreneur in Michigan

Milan was bypassed by a new railway that took traffic from the canal and affected local trade. As a result, Sam Edison moved to Port Huron, Michigan, where he set up a lumber and grain business. Soon afterwards, he sent for his family.

Young Edison did not start school until he was eight, perhaps because of scarlet fever and other illnesses. Three months later, he walked out when his teacher told him that his brain was "addled." His mother was so indignant that she decided to teach him at home.

He made rapid progress. By ten, he was reading, or was having read to him, Gibbon's *Decline and Fall of the Roman Empire*, the *Dictionary of Sciences* and much of Shakespeare and Dickens. He seems to have had little affection for his father. "My mother was the making of me," he said later.

Without realizing it, Thomas was also educating himself. He was passionately interested in electricity and had a simple laboratory in the cellar. Here he carried out one of his earliest experiments. Hoping to generate electricity, he tied two cats together, attached wires to their legs, and rubbed their backs. The attempt failed but it is a good example of the enterprise, originality, and insistence on practical experiment that was to make him one of the greatest inventors in history.

Sam Edison's business did not flourish in Michigan. To help the family budget, Mrs. Edison allowed Thomas to take a job on the Grand Trunk Railroad when he was only twelve. He became a "candy butcher" on the daily train linking Port Huron with Detroit, the state capital, which then had a population of 25,000. Thomas was not paid; his income came from the profit on the sweets, popcorn, and newspapers he sold to the passengers.

Each morning, Thomas joined the train at seven A.M. and arrived at Detroit some three hours later. After replenishing his stocks, he studied books on

Scan here for an inspirational video about Edison's mother:

chemistry, mechanics, and manufacturing at the public library. He spent hours on Newton's *Principles* but finally abandoned it. "It gave me a distaste for mathematics from which I have never recovered," he said later. At four-thirty P.M., he caught the train back to Port Huron.

Thomas was a highly successful candy butcher. He was cheeky and sometimes gave less than he should have, but his open intelligent face and winning manner made him popular with both passengers and railway workers.

When two more trains were added to the run, he hired assistants to sell candy on them. He bought fruit and butter from farmers, carried

Thomas around the age of fourteen, when he worked as a candy butcher on the local Grand Trunk Railroad.

them on the train without paying freight charges, and sold them in the state capital. He set up a stall in Port Huron where yet another assistant sold fresh vegetables he had brought from Detroit.

Thomas had a sharp eye for profit. The American Civil War was now raging. By hanging around the office of the *Detroit Free Press*, he got advance news of the paper's contents. On April 7, 1862, the Battle of Shiloh was fought with a reported 60,000 casualties. A friendly **telegraph** operator wired a brief announcement to stations along the line. Placards were put up saying that further

The Grand Trunk Railroad operated numerous routes in Michigan, Illinois, Indiana, and Ohio. The main line ran from Chicago to Port Huron, Michigan, which was a hub for other railroad lines that went to Detroit as well as major cities on the East Coast and Canada.

details could be obtained from newspapers available on the train. By special arrangement with the editor, Edison took 1,000 copies on credit. At the first stop, he sold forty papers instead of the usual two. At the next stop, he doubled the price to ten cents and sold 150 instead of the usual dozen. At Port Huron, he sold the rest to a stampede of customers at twenty-five cents each. His profit for the day was $150.

His next venture was the *Grand Trunk Herald*, a single-sheet weekly newspaper. He wrote, edited, and printed it in the baggage car of the train, using a secondhand printing press that he had bought with his Shiloh profits. It was a jumble of news, market prices, schedule changes, and jokes. (For example, "'Let me collect myself,' as the man said when he was blown up by a powder mill.") Spelling was poor. "Opision" and "attension" were typical. But he worked the circulation up to 400 copies at eight cents.

Interest in Telegraphy

Bustling and inquisitive, young Thomas Edison had a finger in every pie. One day, he even drove a train. But his main interest was the electric telegraph. It was the latest means of communication and had the kind of glamour we now associate with space technology. As his Shiloh coup had proved, it could bring immediate practical benefits.

For Thomas, it had a special appeal. Perhaps because of a childhood bout with scarlet fever, he had become deaf. From the age of twelve, he never heard a bird sing. But he could hear the telegraph. **Morse code** was transmitted by sending an electric current along a wire. At the receiving end, the current activated an **electromagnet**, which drew a lever toward it. When the current was broken, the lever sprang back to its original position. At each end of its swing, it struck a screw with a sharp click. The time between each pair of clicks depended on how long the sender held down his key, or switch. A long space represented a dash, a short space a dot. Instead of the "dah-dit-dah" familiar with Morse sounders, the sound of the railway telegraph was more like "umpty-iddy-umpty."

Thomas could hear these clicks clearly. In fact, he could hear them better than people with normal hearing because he was not distracted by background noises. He made his own equipment and was soon tapping out messages to a friend along a wire strung between their homes. Eventually, six houses were linked. The system finally broke down when a wandering cow knocked down a pole, became entangled in the wire, and in her panic uprooted all the other poles as well.

In 1862, when he was still fifteen, Thomas was involved in an incident that changed his whole life. Every day, the train stopped at Mount Clemens station for half an hour while extra wagons were attached. These were shunted into position. On the day in question, Thomas saw Jimmy, the two-and-a-half-year-old son of J.U. Mackenzie, the stationmaster, playing on the track. A loose wagon was rolling toward him. Edison hurled himself across its path, knocking the boy to safety. As a reward, Mr. Mackenzie offered to teach him telegraphy.

Thomas seized his chance eagerly. Four nights a week, he stayed with the Mackenzies while an assistant took over the rest of his candy route between Mount Clemens and Port Huron. This left his evenings free for instruction. It is typical of him that he arrived for his first lesson with his own set of instruments, which he had made in the workshop of a friendly gunsmith.

Telegraphy at Mount Clemens consisted mainly of sending and receiving messages about the arrival and departure of trains. At the end of five months, Thomas had learned all that Mr. Mackenzie could teach him. It was enough to qualify him for a thirty-dollar-a-month job as an operator at a Port Huron bookshop that ran a public telegraph service as a sideline.

In these early days of telegraphy, operators drifted from job to job. Thomas was no exception. During the next four years, he tapped his key in almost a dozen offices from Memphis, Tennessee, to Boston, Massachusetts. He lived in cheap rooms, spending his salary on equipment for his never-ending experiments. He became a brilliant operator, but was repeatedly fired for playing pranks or neglecting his work so that he could study

Samuel F. B. Morse (1791–1872) is best known for his invention of the telegraph in 1837 and the development of Morse code the following year.

International Morse Code

A ·—	**N** —·	**1** ·————	**.** ·—·—·—	**=** —···—
B —···	**O** ———	**2** ··———	**,** ——··——	**+** ·—·—·
C —·—·	**P** ·——·	**3** ···——	**?** ··——··	**-** —····—
D —··	**Q** ——·—	**4** ····—	**!** —·—·——	**$** ···—··—
E ·	**R** ·—·	**5** ·····	**'** ·————·	**@** ·——·—·
F ··—·	**S** ···	**6** —····	**"** ·—··—·	
G ——·	**T** —	**7** ——···	**(** —·——·	
H ····	**U** ··—	**8** ———··	**)** —·——·—	
I ··	**V** ···—	**9** ————·	**&** ·—···	
J ·———	**W** ·——	**0** —————	**:** ———···	
K —·—	**X** —··—		**;** —·—·—·	
L ·—··	**Y** —·——		**/** —··—·	
M ——	**Z** ——··		**_** ··——·—	

SOS ···—··—···	**Break** —··· —·—
New Line ·—·—·	**Closing** —·—· ·—··
New Page ·—·—·	**Shift to Wabun code** —··—·——
New Paragraph —···—	**End of contact** ···
Attention —·—·—	**Understood** ···—·
Error ········	**Invitation for named station to transmit** —·—·——
Wait ·—···	**Invitation for any station to transmit** —·—

Morse code became the standard for transmitting messages over the telegraph in the nineteenth century. Letters and numbers are represented by short and long breaks—"dots" and "dashes."

or work on some technical problem. He was shabby and untidy in appearance. A colleague of those days said that he looked like "a veritable hay-seed," or country bumpkin.

From Port Huron, he crossed over to Canada and took a job as a night operator at Stratford Junction railway station some forty miles away. To make sure he stayed awake, he had to send a brief signal to headquarters at regular intervals. Traffic was light and he much preferred to take catnaps so that he would be fresh for his private experiments next day. He rigged up a clock mechanism to trigger a device that sent off the signals automatically. Headquarters failed to get a reply when they called his station immediately after one of these signals. A supervisor was sent to investigate and the game was up.

Thomas was given another chance. Shortly afterward, he was told to stop a train at his station. He should have stopped it and then telegraphed confirmation. Instead, he sent the confirmation first. When he tried to stop the train, he was too late. It had passed through.

Meanwhile, a train traveling in the opposite direction had been allowed to leave the next station down the single-track line. If the drivers had not seen each other's lights and pulled up in time, he would have been responsible for a serious accident. Realizing that his negligence was a serious offence under Canadian law, he crossed back into the United States.

Frustrated Inventor

Thomas Edison was still only seventeen. He worked for short periods as a telegraphist at Adrian, Michigan, Fort Wayne, Indiana, and Indianapolis before graduating to the press desk of the Western Union office at Cincinnati—all in a single year. Western Union was the giant company that ran most of America's telegraph services.

By now, Thomas was a first-class operator and could work at forty-five words per minute. He simplified his style of handwriting so that he could take down messages quickly and legibly. He was earning $105 a month.

Nothing could dampen his zest for invention. He devised electric rat traps and cockroach killers to get rid of the vermin that infested his rooms. In Cincinnati, as a prank he wired up the basin in which railway workers washed. As soon as they dipped their hands in the water, they got a violent shock.

More jobs followed in Nashville and Memphis, Tennessee, and in Louisville, Kentucky. Thomas lived frugally, wearing old clothes and cracked shoes. His salary disappeared in "loans" to his spendthrift colleagues or in the purchase of even more elaborate equipment. He had all sorts of ideas for improving the telegraph. He thought up methods of boosting electric current so that messages could be sent over longer distances. He built a device that recorded fast, incoming messages on paper tape that could be played back at a more leisurely speed later. He used this secretly at Indianapolis when faced with a flood of high-speed press messages. All went well until he fell two hours behind and complaints poured in. The manager found his gadget and banned it.

At Louisville, he was at the point of perfecting a **duplex** system by which two messages could be sent at the same time on a single wire, but the manager forbade him to experiment with the office equipment. Thomas felt so frustrated that he quit his job. He planned to emigrate to Brazil, and after a farewell visit to his parents at Port Huron, got as far as New Orleans before being put off by bad reports about the country. An operator he had known at Cincinnati then told him of a vacancy in the Western Union office at Boston, Massachusetts.

Thomas Edison was now twenty-one. He was keener than ever to work on his inventions and Boston had a light engineering industry that would increase his

PATENT KING

Thomas Edison's first patented invention was the automatic vote recorder, in 1869. He would ultimately be granted a total of 1,093 United States patents, a record number for one person that still stands. He also earned several hundred foreign patents from Great Britain, France, Germany and other countries. Most foreign patents were similar to the American ones.

scope considerably. After a journey of four days and nights, he started work as a telegraphist at five-thirty P.M. on the day of his arrival.

When he was off duty, he had access to a public library with more than a quarter of a million volumes. He also browsed in second-hand bookshops. "He bought," said Milton Adams, an operator with whom he shared a room, "the whole of Faraday's works on electricity, brought them home at three o'clock in the morning and read assiduously until I rose. Tom's brain was on fire with what he had read. He suddenly remarked to me, 'I've got so much to do and life is so short, that I am going to hustle.'"

The hustler had already made himself known in the many workshops that specialized in making scientific instruments. He arranged to spend his free time with Charles Williams Jr. so that he could continue with his experiments. Here too he met small capitalists who were on the lookout for likely inventions to invest in. He persuaded one of these to advance him $500 in return for a half share in his duplex telegraph. Another backed his idea for an electric vote recorder with $100. For the first time in his life, Edison had capital. He quit his job at Western Union and became a full-time inventor.

Everything went wrong. His vote recorder, a device by which members of Congress could vote simply by pressing a button on their desks, worked perfectly. But when he demonstrated it in Washington, D.C., the chairman of Congressional committees told him, "It's the last thing on earth we want here. **Filibustering** and delay in the counting of votes are often the only means we have for defeating bad legislation."

He borrowed a further $800 to develop his duplex telegraph. When it failed to work, he was left with a heavy debt.

His third main invention of these days worked and also filled a real demand. Stockbrokers needed minute-by-minute information about stock market prices. In New York, Dr. Samuel S. Laws devised a machine that showed gold prices on the dials of indicators placed in subscribers' offices. These were linked to a central transmitter by telegraph wires.

Edison's "stock ticker" was a distinct improvement. Though not the first of its kind, it showed prices not on a dial but printed out on a continuous strip of paper. It covered not just gold but any commodity or share on which information was required. It was called a "ticker" because of the noise it made.

Edison employed several men to help make the machines and soon had some thirty subscribers. Unwisely, he sold out the **patent** rights just as it was about to become profitable.

He decided it was time to move on again. Leaving all his equipment behind in Boston, he borrowed enough money to pay his boat fare to New York. He could scarcely have foreseen the spectacular successes that awaited him.

TEXT-DEPENDENT QUESTIONS

1. Where was Thomas Alva Edison born?
2. What job did Thomas take when he was twelve years old?
3. What is Morse code?
4. Why did a representative of Congress decline to invest in Edison's vote-recording machine?

RESEARCH PROJECT

Using your school library or the internet, find out about the Samuel Morse, who invented the telegraph in the 1840s. Write a two-page biography of Morse, and share it with your class.

Portrait of Thomas Edison, 1870s.

emboss—to carve, mold, or stamp a design on a surface, so that it stands above the surface.

frock coat—a knee-length, double-breasted coat that was popular among fashionable men during the 1860s and 1870s.

mimeograph—a machine that makes copies of an original document.

telegraph relay—a device that amplified electrical signals carried on a telegraph line, detecting a weak signal and using a battery to strengthen it so that it could be picked up by a receiver farther down the line.

CHAPTER 2

The Robber Barrons

Edison arrived in New York one morning in May 1869. The Civil War had ended four years before and business in the city was booming. Edison, by contrast, was literally penniless. His only assets were a small but growing reputation in the world of telegraphy and a breathtaking resourcefulness.

Wandering hungrily from the wharf, he looked through a warehouse window. Inside, a tea taster was at work. Playing the country bumpkin, Edison walked in and asked him what he was doing. "Could you spare me a packet so that I could try it for myself?" he begged. Within a few minutes, he had persuaded a nearby café proprietor to exchange his packet of tea for a cup of coffee and a plate of apple dumplings.

His hope of a bed disappeared when he found that his only friend in the city had gone away. For a day and a night, he walked the streets. The next morning, he found a telegrapher friend who lent him a dollar. He lived on this for several days.

His next call was at the offices of the Gold Indicator Company, which had been formed by Samuel Laws to operate his information service for brokers. Frank Pope, the company's chief engineer, proved friendly. He gave Edison permission to sleep in the battery room and allowed him to spend as much time as he wished studying the complicated machinery of the indicator.

One day, it broke down. Pope was unable to locate the problem. Desperate for news, the stockbrokers sent messenger boys who clamored in the outer office. Laws was in a panic. Edison appeared, glanced quickly over the machinery, and told him, "There is a contact spring which has broken and fallen between two cog-wheels. This prevents the gear from moving."

The fault was soon put right. Laws was so grateful that he offered Edison a job as Pope's assistant. Shortly afterward, Pope left to form his own company and Edison became the chief engineer at a salary of $300 a month. He soon found ways to improve the gold indicator, mainly by adding to it a device for printing out stock prices. An electric current from the central office activated two electromagnets on each of the receiving machines. One electromagnet operated a wheel **embossed** with type, turning it to the letter or numeral required. The second electromagnet brought the paper tape sharply into contact with this wheel. It then carried the paper forward one space, ready for the next letter. The ink came from a felt roller that brushed against the rotating wheel.

The new equipment was so successful that Western Union bought out the Gold Indicator Company. General Marshall Lefferts, the head of Western Union, wanted to keep Edison on. Edison preferred to leave and set up a new company with Pope and J. W. Ashley (editor of *The Telegrapher*) specializing in electrical engineering and inventions. Pope looked after the business side and Ashley gave it free publicity in his magazine.

MORSE TRANSMITTER, about 1850

This is an 1850 key-operated telegraph transmitter.

Scan here to learn how a telegraph works:

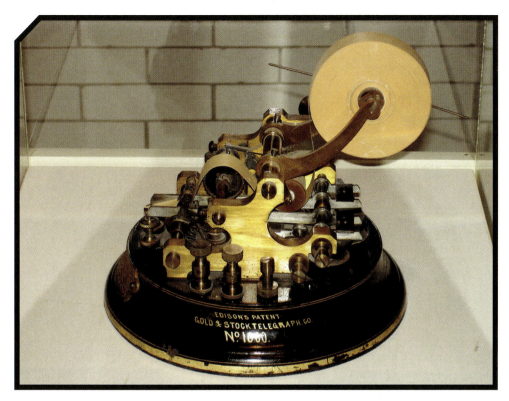

Edison's gold and stock ticker.

A Busy Inventor

Lodging with the Popes in Elizabeth, New Jersey, Edison rented a tiny workshop in Jersey City. He worked harder than ever, rising at six A.M. to catch the seven A.M. train. He stayed at his bench until after midnight. The Popes' home was a half-mile walk from the station. It was a bitter winter. "Many were the occasions when I nearly froze," he said.

The result of this work was a device for transmitting the prices of gold and silver by telegraph. Subscribers could rent a machine for only $25 a week, a point that General Lefferts was quick to notice. He bought up the invention for $15,000, of which Edison received $5,000.

Edison had now been in New York little more than a year. During that time, he had patented seven separate inventions, most of them small technical improvements on the ticker. He now decided to set up on his own. Lefferts bought some of his minor inventions for Western Union, then asked Edison to fix a problem in an earlier ticker that was still widely used. From time to time, it "ran wild" and printed nonsensical figures. Mechanics then had to visit every subscriber to readjust their machine. It might be several hours before the system was working again. Lefferts asked if Edison could devise a way to readjust all the machines at the same time from the central transmitter.

It took three weeks for Edison to find a solution. Lefferts then asked how much he wanted for his work to date. Edison wasn't sure—he wanted to ask for $5,000, but was afraid that figure was too high. Wisely, he replied, "I'd rather you made me an offer." Lefferts proposed $40,000, which Edison accepted immediately, trying not to look surprised.

EDISON'S LETTER HOME

Thomas Edison's success at selling his inventions meant that he could send money home to his parents in Port Huron, to help them financially. Soon after selling his improved stock transmitter to Western Union, Edison wrote the following letter to his father:

"I. C. Edison writes me that mother is not very well and that you have to work very hard. I guess you had better take it easy after this. Don't do any hard work and get mother anything she desires. You can draw on me for money. Write me and say how much money you will need till June and I will send the amount on the first of that month. Give love to all the folks. Is Truey still with you?

Your affec son Thos A."

Edison now set up as a manufacturer, as Western Union had ordered 1,200 stock tickers, worth half a million dollars. The firm was called Edison and Unger because Lefferts had insisted that he take on William Unger, a Western Union man, as partner. Edison rented workshops in Newark, New Jersey, purchased machinery, and hired workmen. His chief assistant was John Ott, who at twenty-one was three years younger than Edison. Under him were two Germans, a Swiss, and an Englishman, all highly skilled mechanics. The total work force was about fifty.

When meeting his business associates, Edison now wore a silk hat and **frock coat**. But in the factory he dressed like a tramp. He supervised his men personally, expecting them to put in as many hours as he did himself. When a $30,000 batch of equipment developed a fault, he locked them up for sixty hours until they had tracked it down. The men put up with it because it was fun

Edison's factory on Ward Street in Newark, 1873.

On Christmas Day 1871, Thomas Edison married sixteen-year-old Mary Stilwell. According to legend, Edison spent the whole afternoon and most of his wedding night working in his laboratory.

to work for him. He gave generous bonuses when things went well. Or he would suddenly take his men off on a fishing expedition. He himself spent long hours in his laboratory/study in the top story of the building. He was now taking out patents by the dozen—thirty-eight in 1872, twenty-five in 1873.

Great changes were taking place in his private life. His mother had died soon after he opened his factory and his father, now a grumbling failure, married a dairymaid.

Edison himself was attracted to one of his workers, sixteen-year-old Mary Stilwell. She was pretty and demure. Edison proposed, bought a house, and married her on Christmas Day, 1871. It is said that he rushed back to his laboratory only an hour after the service and became so absorbed that he stayed until midnight. They nicknamed their first two children—Marion and Thomas—Dot and Dash.

Money Management

Edison was little interested in money for its own sake. He wanted it only so that he could buy the things he needed for his work. He had two hooks in his office—one for unpaid bills, the other for outstanding accounts. "This saved the humbuggery of bookkeeping, which I never understood," he said. "The arrangement possessed besides the advantages of being cheaper. Notwithstanding this extraordinary method of doing business, my credit was excellent."

This attitude was adequate for a twelve-year-old candy butcher, but not for a man who had to do business with clever and unscrupulous financiers. He was caught between the opposing forces of Western Union and Jay Gould, a cunning, corrupt and ruthless financier who now aimed to dominate American telegraphy.

Edison was still working for Western Union when he was approached by two of Gould's henchmen—George Harrington, a former assistant secretary of the U.S. Department of the Treasury, and Josiah Reiff, who was what we would now call his public relations man. They were directors of the Automatic Telegraph Company, which they were secretly running for Gould. It had been formed to exploit an automatic telegraph invented by George D. Little. The invention had run into trouble and they asked Edison to put it right.

He accepted $40,000 in return for the patent rights on any inventions in connection with the automatic telegraph. He opened another factory, took Joseph T. Murray of Newark as a partner and hired Edward H. Johnson, a young railway engineer, as an assistant.

The automatic telegraph was an instrument that punched paper tape with Morse characters. This tape was then run through a machine that transmitted at several thousand words a minute—a rate much faster than any human telegraphist could achieve. But a special type of paper was needed to record the characters at the receiving end.

One of Edison's assistants said later, "I came in one night and there sat Edison with a pile of chemistries and chemical books that were five feet high when they stood on the floor. He had ordered them from New York, London, and Paris. He studied them day and night. He ate at his desk and slept in his chair. In six weeks he had gone through the books, written a volume of abstracts, made two thousand experiments, and had produced a solution which would record 200 words a minute on a wire 250 miles long. He ultimately succeeded in recording 3,100 words a minute."

Edison now closed down Edison and Unger, the firm that made stock tickers. While continuing to work for the Gould interests, he also patented two copying devices on his own account, the electric pen and the **mimeograph**. More important, he persuaded Western Union to back his idea for a duplex telegraph, which could carry two messages at once along a single wire.

In the spring of 1873, Edison sailed to England to demonstrate his automatic telegraph. For various reasons, the British Post Office did not buy the patent rights. When he returned home in June, the United States was plunged into an economic depression.

Edison had always borrowed heavily to finance his work. Now, all his creditors were demanding payment. Unless he could raise money quickly, his workshops and equipment would have to be sold.

The duplex telegraph was his main hope. He was already thinking of developing it into a quadruplex, by which four messages could be passed at the same time. Basically, the idea was to use two currents of different strengths in each direction. There were two sending and two receiving instruments at each end. Each was adapted to respond only to a current of a particular strength flowing in a particular direction. Preliminary tests gave promising results.

Unfortunately, Western Union itself was economizing because of the depression. All through 1873, they refused to back Edison further. The following year, it became clear that they faced severe competition from the Automatic Telegraph Company, which was using Edison's automatic telegraph. They decided to go ahead with the quadruplex, but only on the understanding that Edison should take as his partner George Prescott, Western Union's chief engineer. Prescott did none of the work but he was to receive half the proceeds. Using Western Union workshops, equipment, and telegraphers, Edison soon perfected his quadruplex. He and Prescott formally agreed to sell it to Western Union.

That should have been the end of his difficulties. But they became even worse. Western Union refused to pay him for his work and creditors were threatening to sell up his home. He needed $10,000 immediately.

At this point, Western Union applied for an injunction against the Automatic Telegraph Company to stop them using the **telegraph relay**, on which

Western Union held patent rights. The relay strengthened signals that became weak when sent over long distances. Without it, A.T.C. would be out of business. Harrington asked Edison to devise an alternative. He did so and got $10,000 as an advance payment on the patent rights. This saved his home.

He was still desperately short of money. Western Union advanced him $5,000, which paid off his most pressing debts. Though the quadruplex would clearly save many millions of dollars by enabling one line to do the work of four, they refused to discuss further payment.

General T. T. Eckert was then general superintendent of Western Union. He heard of Edison's plight and told Jay Gould, who immediately offered Edison $30,000 as an advance for his share of the

American financier Jay Gould (1835–92) acquired great wealth during the 1860s through innovative—and often fraudulent—manipulations of railroad stock. He is among the most notable of the "Robber Barons" of the era. In 1875 Gould entangled Edison in his secret scheme to build a telegraph network that would compete with Western Union. Edison regretted the association, which resulted in years of litigation.

quadruplex rights. A tenth of the profits made by the quadruplex would follow. Exasperated by Western Union's delays, Edison accepted. Eckert defected to Gould, who now came into the open as the power behind A.T.C. He bought it up and merged it with his Atlantic and Pacific Telegraph Company, promising to make Edison chief electrician. Edison's share of the quadruplex profits was to come from Atlantic and Pacific stock. The job did not materialize. The stock proved worthless. After a final protest to Gould, Edison told him that he would work henceforth only for Western Union, which "was only too glad to get him back."

Western Union asked the courts to cancel Edison's agreement with Gould so that they alone could use the invention. Their lawyers denounced Edison as a "professor of duplicity and quadruplicity" who had bitten the hand that fed him. Yet only four years later, the president of Western Union admitted in his annual report that the invention was "one of the most important in telegraphy and had saved the company $600,000 annually."

Edison spent his $30,000 advance from Gould in developing an octuplex, which he hoped would carry eight messages simultaneously. "This," he said, "I never completed." He now gave up manufacturing and left the world of finance to the robber barons. Wisely, he returned to his true vocation: industrial invention.

From now on, he would head teams of experts and so be able to work on many projects at the same time. Invention would no longer be the monopoly of lonely geniuses. It would become the concerted effort of scores, perhaps hundreds, of well-trained scientists and technicians. Thus Thomas Edison established a pattern for technological innovation in modern society that continues to this day.

TEXT-DEPENDENT QUESTIONS

1. Who did Edison stay with when he arrived in New York City in 1869?

2. How much did Western Union pay Edison for his work adjusting their stock ticker?

3. What nicknames did Tom and Mary Edison give to their two children, Marion and Thomas?

RESEARCH PROJECT

Construct a simple circuit to understand how a telegraph works. Materials you will need include a 9-volt battery, an electric buzzer with red and black wire leads, and electrical tape. Connect the black wire to the negative terminal of the battery, using a piece of tape to hold it in place. Touch the red wire to the positive terminal. This will complete the circuit, and the buzzer will sound. Holding the wire on the positive terminal will create a long sound (a Morse code "dash"); quickly touching and lifting will make a short sound (a "dot"). Using the chart of international Morse code pictured in this chapter, send a message using your simple circuit.

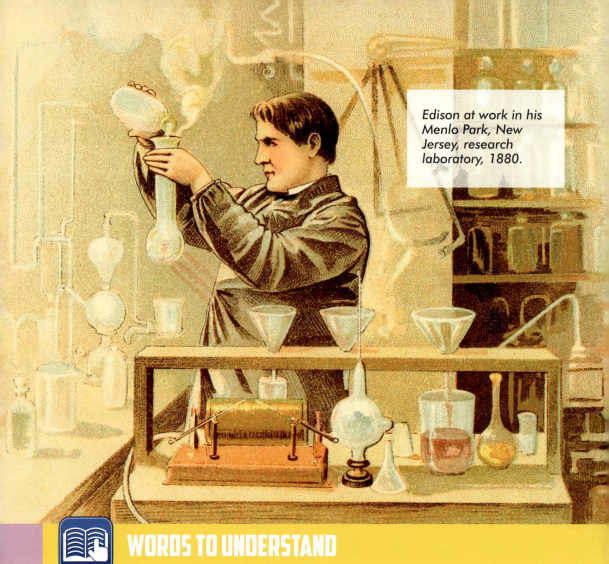

Edison at work in his Menlo Park, New Jersey, research laboratory, 1880.

WORDS TO UNDERSTAND

circuit—the path of an electric current.

crank—a handle for turning a shaft.

diaphragm—a vibrating disc, used in a telephone or microphone.

microphone—device for changing sound waves into electrical energy.

pirate—to infringe on a patent without permission.

resistance—opposition to the passage of an electric current.

royalty—payment for use of someone else's patent.

transformer—device for changing the voltage of an electric current.

CHAPTER 3

The Wizard of Menlo Park

The commissioner of the New York Patent Office once referred to Edison as "that young man in New Jersey who has made the path to the Patent Office hot with his footsteps." He might be working on as many as forty-five devices at the same time. He sold them for large sums of money, which he spent almost immediately on further experiments.

Harassed by the visitors who thronged his New Jersey workshops, he built new premises at Menlo Park, a small hamlet in remote, lightly wooded country twenty-four miles from New York City. "When the public tracks me out here," he said, "I shall simply have to take to the woods."

His father came down from Port Huron to superintend the building. The main workshop was 100 feet long and 35 feet wide. It had two stories. The ground floor housed lathes, punches, drills, and milling machines powered by an 80 horsepower engine, as well as a wide variety of electrical apparatus. The first floor was an experimental laboratory with more electrical equipment, microscopes, air pumps, and every type of chemical and mineral that might be needed. There was a large library of the latest science books.

"The wizard of Menlo Park" was a new type of inventor. He had little in common with either the cranky individualist of legend or the academic interested only in science for its own sake. He was wholeheartedly commercial. He might be the inspirer, but he was also the head of a team. Menlo Park was the first industrial research laboratory in the world.

The nucleus of his team was the band of technicians he had first enrolled at Newark. Edward Johnson looked after the business side. In 1878, Edison hired Francis R. Upton, a Princeton graduate who had studied under the eminent German scientist Hermann von Helmholtz, to work on mathematical problems.

They put in long hours. They were keen to do so, because they enjoyed working for Edison. He had a nickname for everyone. Upton's, for instance, was "Culture." Together with the Edison family and their three African-American servants, the laboratory staff soon outnumbered the other inhabitants of Menlo Park. It became known as "Edison Village."

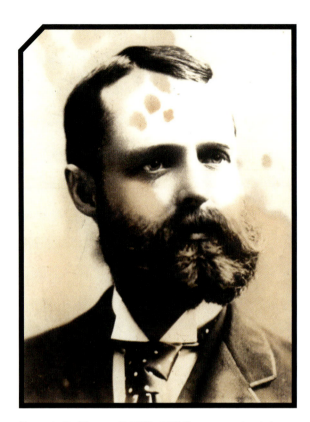

Francis R. Upton (1852–1921) was a physicist and mathematician who became one of Edison's most trusted associates at Menlo Park.

It is impossible to describe all the inventions that poured out of Edison's laboratory. Many were technical improvements on the telegraph. A tasimeter measured heat so precisely that it reacted to a gas jet 100 away. An odorscope measured smells that were otherwise undetectable. A tripod-mounted megaphone fitted with twin trumpets and ear tubes enabled people to speak to each other across several miles.

Thomas Edison with the engineers and technicians of his Menlo Park workshop, c 1880. Edison is under the central arch, leaning against the support with his hands in his pockets.

Two groups of inventions dominated Edison's attention during these years—those concerned with the telephone and phonograph, and those to do with electric light.

Improving the Telephone

Edison did not invent the telephone. That honor clearly belongs to Alexander Graham Bell of Salem, Massachusetts. He filed the patent on February 14, 1876, beating a rival inventor, Elisha Gray of Chicago, by only a few hours.

Bell's telephone had an iron disc, or **diaphragm**, which vibrated when someone spoke into it. Behind the disc was a magnet surrounded by a coil of wire. Movements of the disc set up currents of electricity in the coil of wire. This is called "electromagnetic induction."

Bell's telephone, used in a transmission that took place between Boston and Salem, Massachusetts, on November 26, 1876. To send a message, Bell spoke into the round wooden mouthpiece on the left of the device. This caused the iron diaphragm (the black disk mounted on the other side of the mouthpiece) to vibrate, inducing a fluctuating current in the two electromagnets that face it (wrapped with white fabric). The current could be transmitted over wires to a similar instrument that acted as a receiver. Edison soon patented improvements to the transmitter that were widely adopted.

The electricity flowed along a wire to the receiver at the other end. It passed into a coil of wire and varied the strength of a magnet inside. The varying strength of the magnet set up vibrations in an iron disc. These vibrations corresponded to those of the first iron disc and so were heard as speech.

Bell's telephone had serious drawbacks. There was only one instrument at each end and this had to be used for both sending and receiving. Even when messages were shouted, they could be heard only faintly, and the words were often drowned out by hisses and crackles. The maximum range of Bell's telephone was only about two miles. Even so, there was widespread public interest in the new invention. Concerned about competition, Western Union asked Edison to devise an alternative.

The job was especially difficult for him because of Edison's deafness. He often had to ask colleagues to listen for him, though sometimes he could "hear" by feeling the vibrations with his teeth. On the other hand, deafness had its advantages. It made him work to get a loud, clear sound that even he could hear.

He had a reputation for solving every problem put to him. The telephone was no exception. He used a battery to boost the strength of the signal and linked it with a **transformer**, which stepped it up even further. The necessary variation in strength had to come from a variable **resistance**, which somehow had to correspond to the sound waves of the human voice.

Edison sometimes thought out the solution to a problem. At other times, he worked by trial and error. Now, he was looking for a substance whose ability to carry electricity would vary according to the pressure placed upon it by

EDISON'S HEARING

Thomas Edison was not completely deaf, but a bout of scarlet fever in childhood left him extremely hard of hearing. Otherwise, Edison was in robust health. He regarded his deafness as an asset that helped his concentration, rather than a liability. He was not distracted by background noises, and did not have to listen to small talk. "Freedom from such talk gave me an opportunity to think out my problems," he wrote in old age. "I have no doubt that my nerves are stronger and better to-day than they would have been if I had heard all the foolish conversation and other meaningless sounds that normal people hear. The things that I have needed to hear I have heard."

Edison's Embossing Translating Telegraph, designed in 1876 and built early in 1877 at Menlo Park, New Jersey. This device was able to record telegraph messages so they could be played back later. Lessons Edison learned from developing this invention would assist with subsequent work on the telephone and phonograph.

the vibrations of the iron disc. He tried some 2,000 different chemicals before finding the most suitable—carbon. He placed it in the form of a button between two metal plates behind the metal disc and incorporated it into the **circuit**. He patented his transmitter—really a **microphone**—in February 1878.

It was an immediate success. It transmitted the sound of a voice loud and clear over hundreds of miles. But it was only a transmitter. It had to be used in conjunction with a Bell receiver. Even so, Western Union bought the rights for $100,000.

Two rival networks were set up—the Bell System based in Boston and the American Speaking Telephone Company, a subsidiary of Western Union, based in New York. The legal position was complicated. In essence, Bell owned the receiver and **pirated** Edison's transmitter. The American Speaking Telephone Company owned Edison's transmitter and pirated Bell's receiver.

It was an impossible situation. Western Union decided to leave the telephone field to Bell. They handed over Edison's transmitter and their own telephone network in return for payments that eventually came to $3.5 million. Edison profited from this deal, as well as from foreign patent rights and further development work that netted him $250,000.

Recording and Playing Sound

Even before completing his work on the transmitter, he had invented an almost equally important device that no one else had ever even thought of—the phonograph, a forerunner of the gramophone.

The idea came to him while working on a repeater for messages in Morse code. This was a continuous tape of wax-coated paper wound around a grooved cylinder. A chisel-shaped stylus made indentations on the paper corresponding to dots and dashes. As in an ordinary telegraph, the movements of the stylus were controlled by the making and breaking of an electric circuit by the operator. The tape could then be run through another machine with a stylus that bounced up and down on the indentations. In doing so, it alternately made and broke a circuit, thus sending out Morse signals.

"I found that when the cylinder carrying the indented paper was turned with great swiftness," wrote Edison, "it gave off a humming noise from the indentations—a musical, rhythmic sound resembling that of human talk heard indistinctly." Edison had an eye for happy accidents. He wondered if human talk really could be reproduced.

The iron disc of the telephone transmitter turned sound waves into vibrations. He fitted it with a stylus touching a strip of wax-coated paper running underneath. "I shouted the words 'Halloo! Halloo!' into the mouth-piece, ran the paper back over the steel point and heard a faint 'Halloo! Halloo!' in return. . . . That's the whole story."

John Kruesi, his best mechanic, was given the job of making a working model at

Edison with his phonograph in 1878 on its first public showing.

a piece-work price of $18. It consisted of a shaft carrying a grooved cylinder covered with tin foil. As the shaft was turned by a hand **crank**, the cylinder traveled across the machine. On one side of it was a recording diaphragm and stylus, on the other a reproducing stylus and diaphragm. Each could be swung into contact with the cylinder as needed.

When it was ready, the staff gathered around for a demonstration. The foreman bet Edison a box of cigars that it would not work. Edison slowly turned the handle and repeated the nursery rhyme "Mary had a little lamb" into the recording diaphragm. Then he wound the cylinder back, swung the reproducing stylus into position, and turned the handle again. His voice was heard clearly repeating the nursery rhyme. "Well," said the foreman, "I guess I've lost."

Edison successfully applied for a patent on his phonograph on December 15, 1877. It would, he said, "be largely devoted to music, either vocal or instrumental—and may possibly take the place of the teacher. It will sing the child to sleep, tell us what o'clock it is, summon us to dinner, and warn the lover when it is time to vacate the front porch. As

Drawings of Edison's phonograph and microphone.

a family record, it will be precious, for it will preserve the sayings of those dear to us and even receive the last messages of the dying. It will enable the children to have dolls that really speak, laugh, cry and sing, and imitation dogs that bark, cats that meow, lions that roar, and roosters that crow. It will preserve the voices of our great men and enable future generations to listen to speeches by a Lincoln or a Gladstone. Lastly, the phonograph will perfect the telephone and revolutionize present systems of telegraphy."

Edison's phonograph brought him world fame. He was invited to demonstrate it to U.S. President Rutherford B. Hayes in the White House, the president's official residence in Washington, D.C. The crowds who now bore down on Menlo Park were treated to a repertoire of tricks. Recorded songs were interrupted by cries of "Help! Police! Murder!" By spacing out snippets of repartee on the cylinder, Edison was able to hold a conversation with the machine as he turned the handle.

A company was formed to manufacture phonographs. Edison was paid an advance of $10,000 against a **royalty** of 20 percent on every machine sold. They were set up in arcades where masses paid to hear them. But not for long. The sound quality was poor. The cylinders played for little more than a minute and quickly wore out. Edison himself was disappointed that the device was not good enough to use as an office dictating machine. The phonograph, it seemed, was just a passing novelty. He turned his attention to other things.

For a short video on how Edison's phonograph works, scan here:

TEXT-DEPENDENT QUESTIONS

1. Why did Edison build a new laboratory in Menlo Park, New Jersey?
2. Who invented the telephone?
3. What was the American Speaking Telephone Company?
4. What nursery rhyme did Edison record and play back for his staff to test the phonograph?

 RESEARCH PROJECT

Read the article "The Great 'Hello' Mystery is Solved," to learn how Thomas Edison coined the modern-day telephone greeting. Available at: http://www.nytimes.com/1992/03/05/garden/great-hello-mystery-is-solved.html.

The battery and control room in the first Edison Electric Lighting Station at Pearl Street in lower Manhattan. This engraving is from 1882.

 WORDS TO UNDERSTAND

arc light—light produced when electric current passes from one terminal to another.

dynamo—a machine for making electricity.

fuse—piece of wire that melts when overloaded. It is placed in a circuit to stop dangerously high current from causing damage.

incandescent light—light produced when electric current causes a filament to glow.

mains—principal wires in distribution of electricity.

voltage—measure of electromotive force, i.e., electrical "pressure."

voltmeter—an instrument for measuring voltage.

CHAPTER 4

Let There Be Light

Though still only thirty-one, Edison was now a national figure. Strongly built and of medium height, he had a square, serious face and a hairstyle that reminded people of Napoleon. He usually wore a business suit that, except in studio portraits, was rumpled and even shabby. This is presumably because of the long hours he worked. Edison rarely slept more than six hours a night and often made do with catnaps at his desk.

In the summer of 1878, Edison went on a rare vacation to the Rocky Mountains with a party of scientists. The most important outcome was a suggestion by his friend, Professor George Barker, that he take up the problem of electric light.

It was not a new idea. Sir Humphry Davy, an English chemist, had demonstrated an **arc light** as early as 1808. This was produced when a powerful current of electricity leapt across the gap between two carbon points. In 1831, Michael Faraday, another English chemist, invented a **dynamo** that generated electricity in sufficient quantities to keep these lights going. Since then, arc lights had been used in English lighthouses, Paris streets, and even a few American stores.

"At the time," wrote Edison, "I was more or less at leisure, because I had just finished working on the carbon button telephone, and this electric-light idea took possession of me. It was easy to see what the thing needed: it wanted to be sub-divided. The light was too bright and too big. What we wished for was little lights, and a distribution of them in people's houses in a manner similar to gas."

From the very beginning, then, Edison was thinking on a vast scale. He aimed at nothing less than a complete system of electric lighting—a central power station, a generating plant, **mains** and branch lines to distribute electricity, safety **fuses** and electric bulbs in every room of every house, together with meters to measure how much electrical current had been used. He was challenging the huge American gas industry, which gathered in some $150 million a year, mostly by providing home and business lighting in the big cities.

It was easy to subdivide the power. Instead of connecting up the lights "in series" (in a continuous chain), he would wire them "in parallel" (i.e. each would have its own separate leads to the negative and positive wires from the generator). This way, if a lamp failed or was switched off, it would not break the entire circuit, plunging whole areas into darkness. Only that lamp would go out.

The Challenge of the Light Bulb

Inventing a low-powered electric light was much more difficult. What was needed, said Edison, was "a candle that will give a pleasant light, not too intense, which can be turned on and off as easily as gas. Such a candle cannot be made from carbon points, which waste away, and must be regulated constantly while they last. Some composition must be discovered which will be luminous when charged with electricity and that will not wear away."

He was not thinking of getting light from an electric arc, but from a substance that gave a bright glow when heated by electricity. This is called an **incandescent light**.

On October 5, 1878, Edison applied for a patent on an incandescent lamp with a platinum filament. It fulfilled all his requirements, except that the platinum melted after ten minutes and the lamp had to be replaced. Nevertheless, on the advice of his lawyer, Grosvenor Lowrey, he announced that the problem was largely solved. Moreover, his system would make available electric power for everything from cookers to sewing machines.

His remarks were reported all over the world. Many scientists were scornful. But, as Lowrey had guessed, American financiers took more notice. Gas shares fell. The Edison Electric Light Company was created to back his idea. It gave him

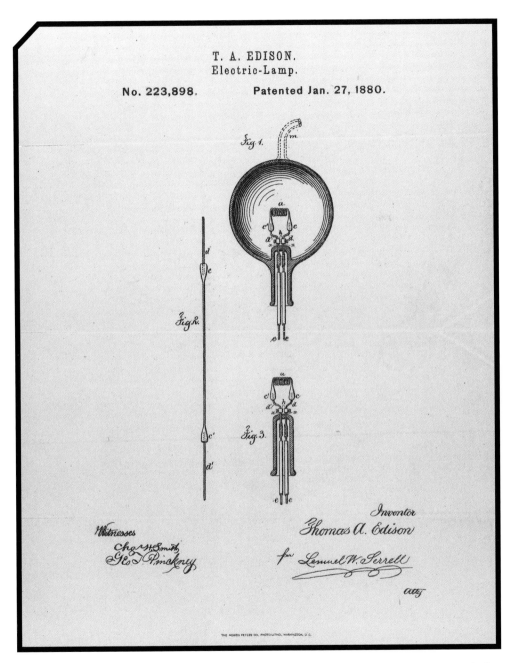

On January 27, 1880, Edison received this historic patent for an incandescent light bulb. His development of a long-burning light bulb would pave the way for electric light to be adopted in cities throughout the world.

Edison did not invent the electric light bulb, but he did produce the first commercially viable bulb by developing a better filament and improving the vacuum within the bulb. This is an example of one of Edison's original light bulbs, which used a carbonized cardboard filament. Later bulbs included filaments produced from bamboo.

$50,000 for research and a large block of shares. In return, it was to have sole rights in his electric lighting inventions over the next five years. The investors were mainly Western Union officials, but J. Pierpont Morgan, a powerful banker, was involved in the company as well.

Rashly, Edison had predicted that he could produce a system in six weeks. It took him well over a year. New buildings went up at Menlo Park—an engine house, a glassblower's shed and an office that also housed a library and a hospitality room for distinguished visitors.

The light bulb was still the main problem. When heated to the point where it gave off a bright light, platinum melted. Carbon, which had a melting point of 3,500 degrees centigrade, burned out long before the right temperature was reached, even in a vacuum.

He tried dozens of other materials, nearly blinding himself with the brief flash given off by nickel. Then he tried platinum again. The newly invented Sprengel pump enabled him to obtain a much higher vacuum than was previously possible. This had several effects. Any material heated in a vacuum lasted longer before burning out. Also, it was possible to extract from the incandescent

Scan here to learn more about Edison's development of the light bulb:

materials hidden gases trapped inside them. This made them still more resistant to burning out. It hardened them, too, so that they were less liable to melt. By April 1879, Edison had developed a much brighter platinum light. But it still fused far too quickly. He now intensified his search for a suitable alternative. Some 1,600 materials were tested.

Developing the Power System

Meanwhile, "Culture" Upton was largely responsible for calculating the size (and therefore the cost) of the copper mains required to carry the amount of electricity needed to make hundreds of thousands of lamps light up.

At the same time, Edison was working on an improved dynamo. He needed one that would provide a constant **voltage** for all parts of his system. It also had to be economical. By the middle of 1879, he had found the type of dynamo he required. It was driven by steam. Instead of the usual belt drive, which wasted a good deal of energy, the shaft of the steam engine itself drove the dynamo. Its voltage was a fairly steady 110.

Edison went back to the bulb. None of the materials tried had proved successful. New calculations by Upton showed that the lamp had to use even less power than he had previously thought. He needed a material, therefore, with a high electrical resistance. For maximum economy, it had to be only one sixty-fourth of an inch thick and six inches long.

Theoretically, carbon was ideal but, as previously noted, it tended to burn out. However, Edison's new technique for removing hidden gases made this less likely. He experimented with carbon again, this time in the form of soot, mixed with tar and molded by hand into fine threads, or filaments.

Tension rose high. Edison's money was running out and his backers were becoming impatient. He was now sleeping less than four hours a day. When his men flagged, he ordered food and wine for a party. They sang or listened to recordings of comic songs on the phonograph.

The soot filaments burned for up to two hours. He felt he was on the right track and looked for other forms of carbon. The breakthrough came from a reel of ordinary sewing cotton. He placed a hairpin-shaped length in a mold, heated it in a furnace for five hours, and carefully took out the thread of carbon that remained. It broke immediately.

Edison persevered. "All night, Bachelor, my assistant, worked beside me," he wrote. "The next day and the next night again, and at the end of that time we had produced one carbon out of an entire spool. Having made it, it was necessary to take it to the glass-blower's house. With the utmost precaution, Bachelor took up the precious carbon, and I marched after him, as if guarding a mighty treasure. To our consternation, just as we reached the glass-blower's bench the wretched carbon broke.

African-American draftsman and inventor Lewis Latimer (1848–1928) was an American inventor and draftsman. He drew the illustrations for Alexander Graham Bell's telephone patent application in 1876, and received a patent in 1881 for an improved process for manufacturing light bulb filaments. He was hired by Edison Electric Light Company in 1884, and worked with Edison for many years.

"We turned back to the main laboratory and set to work again. It was late in the afternoon before we had produced another carbon, which was again broken by a jeweler's screw-driver falling against it. But we turned back again, and before night the carbon was completed and inserted in the lamp. The bulb was exhausted of air, and the sight we had so long desired to see met our eyes."

This filament burned for forty-five hours on October 11 and 12, 1879. On November 1, Edison applied for a patent. Yet he was still not satisfied. The cotton filament had shown that vegetable fibers were most suitable. Was there another that would be even more effective than cotton? He tried every type he could lay his hands on, from boxwood to human hair. Cardboard turned out to be the best. By Christmas, Menlo Park was ablaze with lights that used burnt cardboard filaments.

Success

After months of secrecy, Edison gave the newspapers a full story. It was a world sensation. Inventors in England, the United States, and many other countries had also been working on incandescent lamps. They now acknowledged defeat. The business world was equally impressed. Shares in the Edison Electric Light Company rose to six times their previous value. More important, the company's investors, who had been uneasy about the many delays, now advanced Edison another $57,000 for development.

Visitors thronged to Menlo Park. On New Year's Eve alone, 3,000 came to wonder at the lights. One of them wrote, "The lamps are about four inches long, small and delicate, and comely enough for use in any apartment. They can be removed from a chandelier is readily as a glass stopper from a bottle and by the same motion. The current is turned on and off by pressing a button."

Not all the visitors were friendly. William E. Sawyer, a rival inventor, drunkenly accused Edison of trickery. Later, he unsuccessfully challenged Edison's patent on the ground that he had filed it first. One gas company sent a saboteur who attempted to put the system out of action by short-circuiting it. Edison had foreseen that this might happen and had protected each group of wires with a safety fuse. Only four bulbs went out.

Edison now faced a host of technical problems in working out a system of distributing electricity from the dynamos in the central generating station. One was economic. "Mains" are the main cables carrying power from the central station to local distribution points. If they were big enough to carry power to 10,000 bulbs, they would cost some quarter of a million dollars in copper alone. Even then, the lights farthest from the generators would be a third less bright than those nearest because of power losses.

The dynamo room in the first Edison Electric Lighting Station at Pearl Street in lower Manhattan, 1882.

He solved both problems at once with his "feeder and main" system. This consisted of feeder wires that took power directly from the dynamos to distribution points on the mains. It cut the cost of copper needed by almost nine tenths. It also kept the power constant throughout the system.

This was only one of dozens of entirely new ideas that poured out of Menlo Park. Edison wanted a lamp filament that lasted longer than the 300 hours expected from burnt cardboard. He tested more than 6,000 vegetable fibers. "Finally," Edison later explained, "I carbonized a strip of bamboo from a Japanese fan, and saw that I was on the right track. But we had a rare hunt finding the real thing. A man went down to Havana, Cuba and the day he got there he was seized with yellow fever and died in the afternoon. I sent a schoolmaster to Sumatra and another fellow up the Amazon. William H. Moore, one of my associates, went to Japan and got what we wanted there. We made a contract with an old Jap to supply us with the proper fiber, and that man went to work and cultivated and cross-fertilized bamboo until he got exactly the quality we required."

In 1880, Henry Villard, a financier who was soon to join the board of Edison Electric, gave Edison a chance to demonstrate his system to a still wider public. Villard owned the S.S. *Columbia*, a ship newly built to link New York with the Pacific Coast via Cape Horn. (The Panama Canal had not yet been built.) Edison installed a complete lighting system for the ship with steam engines, dynamos, and 115 lamps. It was a complete success.

Other trials were more exacting. At Menlo Park, Edison laid eight miles of underground mains, solving as he did so the problem of insulating them against loss of power. He wired the handful of houses in the hamlet and erected

EDISON'S INGENUITY

When Edison opened his dynamo in New York in 1881, he was asked how he knew the amount of electrical current that would be needed to light homes in that area. "Simplest thing in the world," Edison explained. "I hired a man to start in every day about two o'clock and walk through the district noting the number of gas lights burning in the various premises; then at three o'clock he went around again and made more notes, and at four o'clock and up to every other hour to two or three o'clock in the morning. In that way, it was easy enough to figure out the gas consumption of every tenant and of the whole district; other men took other sections."

lampposts along a network of "streets" over half a square mile. When he flung a switch in the central power station, the whole area blazed with the light of 425 lamps.

By now his eyes were on New York. In January 1881, he successfully demonstrated a huge new dynamo powered by a 120-horsepower steam engine.

Edison believed that electricity would replace gas for lighting purposes. It was more convenient and just as cheap. The directors of Edison Electric were less sure. They refused to finance factories to manufacture the necessary equipment. So Edison manufactured it himself. For capital, he either sold his stock in Edison Electric or used it as security for loans.

Three new companies sprang up. At Menlo Park, the Edison Lamp Company was soon producing 1,000 light bulbs a day. In New York, the Edison Machine Works turned out dynamos in an old dockland factory. He also had a third share in another company, which made smaller items of equipment—from fuses to lamp sockets. Together, these companies employed 1,000 men.

Lighting New York City

By now the directors of Edison Electric were beginning to wake up. Perhaps, after all, they could beat the gas companies. Impressed by the thoroughness of Edison's market research and profit forecasts, they got permission from New York City to set up an electric lighting system. They formed a subsidiary, the Edison Illuminating Company of New York, and raised $80,000 to help finance a central station.

Edison moved into a New York hotel with his wife and three children. He rented 65 Fifth Avenue, a luxurious townhouse, for business purposes and quickly had it blazing with electric light. The first district he planned to supply lay to the north of Wall Street, the financial sector. He chose it because it contained every type of property, from hovels to huge business offices.

"I planned out the station and where it ought to go," he said, "but we could not get real estate [land] where it was wanted. It cost us $150,000 for two old

View of New York's City Hall blazing with electric lights, 1904.

buildings down in Pearl Street where we finally settled."

No one had ever set up a central power station before. He encountered unexpected difficulties in getting the steam engines to work together. He had to invent from scratch fuse wire, **voltmeters**, and numerous other items that we now take for granted.

Meanwhile, there were eighteen miles of ditches to dig and mains to lay. "I saw every box poured and every connection made on the whole job," he said. "There was nobody else who could superintend it. I used to sleep nights on piles of pipes at the station."

At three P.M. on September 4, 1882, the lights were finally switched on. There were only 400 of them. It soon became evident that the $600,000 spent so far would not reap quick profits. Bulbs cost a dollar each. Faults often brought blackouts. Some houses caught fire. In one, a man was burned to death. But Edison had shown that his lighting system worked. It was only a matter of time before electric light made gas light as obsolete as the stagecoach.

TEXT-DEPENDENT QUESTIONS

1. What is a filament?
2. What is the benefit of connecting lights to the electrical system in parallel, rather than in series?
3. What company was created to finance Edison's work on electric lighting?
4. How did the SS *Columbia* help publicize Edison's ideas?

RESEARCH PROJECT

Using the internet or your school library, find out more about arc lighting. How is it different from incandescent lighting? What scientists or engineers developed arc lighting? Write a two-page report and share it with your class.

Thomas Edison in his West Orange, New Jersey, laboratory, circa 1901.

WORDS TO UNDERSTAND

alternating current (AC)—an electric current that repeatedly changes its direction or strength, usually at a certain frequency or range of frequencies. AC has an advantage over direct current because it is easy to raise and lower the voltage of such current. It was developed by Nikola Tesla, and became widely adopted over Edison's direct current in the 1890s.

direct current (DC)—electricity that flows in a constant direction, and possesses a voltage with constant polarity, such as the kind of electricity generated by a battery, with definite positive and negative terminals.

radio—wireless telegraphy or telephony.

typhoid fever—a serious disease spread by contaminated food and water that can cause high fevers, headache, internal bleeding, and in severe cases, death.

widower—a man whose wife has died.

CHAPTER 5

Losing Touch

In 1882, Edison seemed set to witness the triumph of his electrical inventions. However, Edison's triumphs were slow in coming. Financiers expected a quick return on the money they invested, but central power stations were expensive and revenue from them low. After two years, Pearl Street had only 500 customers burning some 10,000 lamps. Morgan and the other major shareholders in Edison Electric preferred to invest in railroads and other more profitable industries, rather than spending additional capital to expand the New York lighting system.

There was, however, a steady demand for small electricity-generating plants that could be used to light large buildings, or in small towns without gas light. These were supplied by the Edison Company for Isolated Lighting, and financed through the T.A. Edison Construction Department—both subsidiaries of Edison Electric. Edison's own manufacturing companies were paid for equipment partly in cash and partly in shares in the various power companies set up. They also gave a good deal of credit.

Naturally, the manufacturing companies prospered. In late 1884, Edison successfully fought a move by Edison Electric to take them over. Three years later, the directors of the parent company took the plunge. They agreed to an expansion of Pearl Street and the building of two more central stations in New York. When they came into operation two years later, there were fifty-eight central stations in other cities as well as some 500 isolated plants.

Edison was rich, drawing dividends from both the manufacturing companies and from Edison Electric, in which he still had a minority holding. But he still supervised the work personally. He traveled extensively and was always ready to dirty his hands and his business suit helping his workmen in an emergency.

What he hated were the endless lawsuits in which he became involved. Other inventors—some of them honest, others pirates—repeatedly tried to upset his innumerable patents by claiming that they had thought of them first. Or Edison Electric might itself be fighting rival companies infringing Edison patents.

After giving evidence in one of these cases, Edison wrote, "Waited one hour for the appearance of a lawyer who is to cross-examine me on events that occurred eleven years ago. Went on stand at 11:30. He handed me a piece of paper with some figures on it, not another mark. Asked in a childlike voice if these were my figures, what they were about and what day eleven years ago I made them. This implied compliment to the splendor of my memory was at first so pleasing to my vanity that I tried every means to trap my memory into stating just what he wanted—but then I thought what good is a compliment from a ten-cent lawyer, and I waived back my recollection. A lawsuit is the suicide of time."

Edison now had other problems. His manufacturing companies employed between 2,000 and 3,000 workers. They owned shares worth some $4 million in the companies they supplied. But they were so short of cash that they were barely able to meet new orders. Edison agreed to merge his other companies with Edison Electric.

The new company was to be called the Edison General Electric Company. It was dominated by banker J. Pierpont Morgan. Edison Electric exchanged its own shares for shares in Edison General Electric worth $3.5 million. The manufacturing companies picked up slightly less in shares and cash. Of this, Edison himself collected rather more than half. Further capital expansion left him with a 10 percent share of Edison General Electric. But he was still a director.

In 1892, competition between Edison General Electric and the rival electrical firm of Thomson-Houston led to a price-cutting war. The cost of bulbs fell from a dollar to forty-four cents. Anxious to avoid further losses, Morgan and Charles A. Coffin, head of Thomson-Houston, decided to join forces in a new firm to be called the General Electric Company.

Edison was outraged. He had invented electric lighting. The fortunes of G.E.C.

First floor heavy machine shop in building five of the West Orange laboratory.

rested largely on his own patents. Yet Morgan had not consulted him about the new merger. Even his name had been dropped from the title. Shortly afterward, he sold his shares in G.E.C. and resigned his directorship. He had finished with electric lighting for good.

Heartbreak and New Love

Meanwhile, even greater changes had taken place in his private life. In 1884, his wife, Mary, had died at the age of twenty-nine. It is believed that she died of **typhoid fever**, although her death certificate states that she died of "congestion of the brain." Except at meals and on Sundays she had seen little of her husband because of the long hours Edison spent in his laboratory. Yet, there was a deep affection between them. Though quiet, she had coped well with her swift rise from factory girl to millionaire's wife.

Mina Miller Edison (1865–1947), Thomas Edison's second wife. Edison once wrote that he taught her Morse code while they were dating, so that they could converse secretly by tapping out messages to each other when her family was present. They married on February 24, 1886.

At age thirty-eight, Edison found himself a **widower** with three children. He sent Marion, now thirteen, to a boarding school and arranged for her brothers, Thomas Junior and William Leslie, to live with their mother's sister, Alice, who had married a foreman at Menlo Park.

Edison's friends invited him out to dinner. They took him to concerts and theatres. Early in 1885, while staying at the Woodside, Boston, home of Ezra Gilliland, an old friend who was now working for him, he met Mina Miller, a striking, self-assured girl of eighteen. She was the daughter of a self-made manufacturer of Akron, Ohio. He soon fell in love with her.

"Saw a lady who looked like Mina," he wrote in his diary. "Got thinking about Mina and came near being run over by a street car. If Mina interferes much more, will have to take out an accident policy."

One night, his friends pointed out the beauty of the full moon on the water. "Couldn't appreciate it, was so busy taking a mental triangleation [sic] of the moon, the two sides of the said triangle meeting the base line of the earth at Woodside and Akron, Ohio."

Edison proposed and was accepted. He bought a huge mansion called Glenmont in West Orange, New Jersey, near New York, and had a winter residence built in Fort Myers, Florida. Here he took his bride after a wedding for which the whole of Akron turned out. He had chosen well. Mina bore his long absences patiently. She shone at his side on public occasions. She gave him a daughter, Madeleine, and two sons, Charles and Theodore.

Missed Opportunities

Edison's inventive genius was now blazing less brightly. Compared with his rivals, however, he was still a force to be reckoned with. Ideas never stopped coming. While still working on the elusive light filament, he had found time to

Thomas Edison purchased Glenmont as a wedding present for his bride, Mina Miller, and they lived in this mansion for over forty years. They are buried on the property behind the house.

build an electric locomotive that worked well over two and a half miles of track at Menlo Park. He did not further develop this idea, however, because he was too busy with other things. So he missed out on one of America's fastest-growing industries.

This was, perhaps, the first sign that Edison was losing touch with the mainstream of technological progress. His failure to pursue wireless **radio** transmission was another. It was a natural development of telegraphy. Moreover Edison himself had made three of the basic inventions on which Guglielmo Marconi, the Italian pioneer of radio, was to build. These included the microphone, an antenna that he used for sending signals through space by means of magnetic induction, and an electronic lamp from which the radio valve was eventually developed.

In the 1890s, Edison foresaw the possibilities of the motor car. Steam engines were too cumbersome, but gas engines of the time were unreliable. The future seemed to lie with electric cars, which were already appearing on the streets in fair numbers. What they needed was a light, durable, high-capacity battery that would give them an adequate range.

After ten years, he perfected one. It was to prove useful in industry, in radio transmissions, and in ships—especially submarines. The battery even made a

To learn more about Nikola Tesla, who developed alternating current, scan here:

small profit. But Edison missed out on the enormous motor car market. Ironically, it would be captured in the early twentieth centuries by one of his own engineers, who left to develop a gas engine and later became one of Edison's closest friends. His name was Henry Ford.

Direct Current versus Alternating Current

Edison also turned his back on new methods of distributing electricity. His own equipment was designed for generating and distributing **direct current** (DC) at a voltage of 110. It was safe and it sufficed for his electric lamps. But it was expensive to transmit direct current over long distances, and was not powerful enough to run the heavy industrial machinery that was now being developed.

George Westinghouse, founder of the Westinghouse Electrical and Manufacturing Company, supported a system of **alternating current** (AC). Even at 5,000 or 10,000 volts, it could be transmitted cheaply over huge distances. It was adequate for industry and could be "stepped down" for ordinary lighting purposes. The AC system made the harnessing of Niagara Falls as a source of power possible.

Edison allowed his publicists to sensationalize the alleged dangers of alternating current. Dogs were electrocuted at public lectures. Partly as a result, New York State brought in the "electric chair" as a method of executing murderers. Alternating current was here to stay.

Edison's most spectacular failure was in iron ore crushing. The Appalachian mines that had produced high-grade iron ore were worked out. Transportation costs made the use of Michigan ore uneconomical for the Eastern ironworks. Edison developed a method of crushing low-grade ore and separating iron-rich particles from the sand using magnetism. These were then compressed into blocks so they would be easy to handle. Edison bought or leased land in New Jersey containing an estimated 200 million tons of low-grade ore. He built elaborate works at Ogdensburg and hired 500 men. After ten years, he was ready to fill an order for 10,000 tons for the Bethlehem Steel Company.

Entrepreneur and electrical engineer George Westinghouse Jr. (1846–1914) recognized the potential of alternating current for distributing electricity in the early 1880s. As he developed an electrical distribution system utilizing alternating current in the early 1880s, he came into direct competition with Edison's direct current system. The competition between the two systems became known as the "War of the Currents," and resulted in AC becoming the standard by the early 1890s.

At this point, a scheme was devised for carrying high-grade ore cheaply from Minnesota by rail and boat. Prices dropped sharply. It cost Edison twice as much to produce iron from his process as he could now get from selling them. In 1899, he closed the scheme down. He had lost $2 million and incurred debts of a further $300,000. "We had a hell of a good time spending it," he said.

TEXT-DEPENDENT QUESTIONS

1. What was the purpose of the Edison Company for Isolated Lighting?
2. Why did Thomas Edison sell his shares in the General Electric Company?
3. What innovation did Italian inventor Guglielmo Marconi develop?

RESEARCH PROJECT

Using your school library or the internet, find out about the banker John Pierpont Morgan, who helped to finance Edison's inventions, but also supported some of Edison's rivals and took control of his electric company. Write a two-page report about the relationship between Morgan and Edison, and share your findings with your class.

Edison in his West Orange laboratory, 1911.

WORDS TO UNDERSTAND

anecdote—a short and amusing or interesting real-life story.

anticlimax—a disappointing end to an exciting or impressive series of events.

induction coil—device for increasing the voltage of an electric current.

underinsured—to have inadequate insurance coverage to pay for all the losses or damages that occur in an accident.

CHAPTER 6

Recorded Music and Movies

Edison's main interest was now in research. Having outgrown Menlo Park, he built a large new laboratory half a mile from his home at West Orange, New Jersey. It was a three-story brick building, 250 feet long and 60 feet wide. There were also four single-story buildings as part of the complex, each some 100 feet by 25 feet.

Many of the departments changed their names as Edison's interests changed. In the early 1890s, they included a heavy machine shop, a precision department, a mercury vacuum pump room, a lamp test room, a chemical room, a galvanometer department, an ore-milling department, and a storeroom, as well as a lecture hall, an exhibition hall and a library of 40,000 volumes. Edison was still the go-getting candy butcher at heart. Framed by his desk was the note signed by the editor of the *Detroit Free Press* when he asked for extra copies on the day of the battle of Shiloh: "Give this boy all the papers he wants on credit."

Edison now employed many university-trained scientists. A separate team handled each project. He supervised them all personally. Improvements to his lamps and lighting system were regularly made. Two other innovations eventually made him a multimillionaire.

EDISON'S MUCKERS

One measure of Thomas Edison's genius was that he surrounded himself with educated, hard-working, and dedicated people to help him to develop his patented ideas into workable devices. He called the best of these workers his "muckers." The photo on the opposite page shows key members of the team that worked on Edison's "perfected" phonograph in 1887. Edison is seated in the center, with Fred Ott on the left and the well-dressed George Gouraud on the right. Standing behind them are (left to right) W. K. L. Dickson, Charles Batchelor, Theo Wangemann, John Ott, and Charles Brown.

John Ott (1850–1931) and his younger brother Fred P. Ott (1860–1936) were machinists who worked in Edison's lab in Newark during the 1870s. By 1887 John Ott was the superintendent of the machine shop at the West Orange facility. After finishing work on the phonograph, Fred Ott would be featured in some of the earliest motion pictures produced by Edison, which were filmed in 1894.

Colonel George Gouraud (1842–1912) had won the Medal of Honor while serving with the Union Army during the Civil War. In the 1870s and 1880s, he worked as Edison's agent in Europe, introducing his new electric inventions to foreign leaders and dignitaries.

William Kennedy-Laurie Dickson (1860–1935) was a Scottish inventor who had begun working for Edison at Menlo Park in 1883. After this photo was taken, Edison assigned Dickson the task of developing the first motion-picture device, the Kinetoscope, as well as a camera. Dickson would eventually leave Edison's employ to establish The Biography Company, which would become one of the most prominent American film studios in the early twentieth century.

Charles W. Batchelor (1845–1910) was one of Edison's closest friends and business partners. They had begun working together in 1871, when Edison's laboratory was located in Newark. Batchelor had

been involved in most of Edison's major projects, including telephone improvements and electric lighting. Batchelor became wealthy from his shares of stock in Edison's manufacturing ventures, although he lost a considerable amount in an ore-milling fiasco in Ogdenburg, New Jersey. After the ore company failed, he left Edison's company.

Adelbert Theodor "Theo" Wangemann (1855–1906) was a German musician who went to work for Edison in 1888. He was hired to find the best ways to record music and voice for the phonograph. In 1889 Edison sent Wangemann to Europe with the phonograph, where he demonstrated its operation and recorded many famous singers, musicians, entertainers, and political leaders. The wax cylinders containing these recordings were lost for many years, but were rediscovered in 2012.

Charles A. Brown was a machinist who later worked as Dickson's assistant in the development of the motion picture camera and the Kinetoscope.

Developing the Phonograph

For ten years Edison had regarded the phonograph as a scientific novelty that had few commercial possibilities. In 1886, however, Alexander Bell, the inventor of the telephone, patented an improved machine with a wax-coated cylinder. He called it a "graphophone." Stung into competition, Edison switched over to a solid wax cylinder. He devised a floating stylus and an electroplated "master" record from which a large number of copies could be pressed. An electric motor

The main entrance into Edison's laboratory complex in West Orange, New Jersey, which opened in 1887. The complex included a library, machine shops, chemistry, physics and metallurgical laboratories, and space for experiments. Edison built his manufacturing business around the laboratory complex, which at its peak employed nearly 10,000 people.

was added that would turn the cylinder at a constant speed. By 1888, Edison had a saleable machine.

As so often happened, Edison proved to be a better inventor than businessman. Jesse W. Lippincott, a Pittsburgh glass manufacturer, had already purchased the Bell patents. He now bought Edison's patents, too. Edison received $500,000 and the sole right to make the phonographs.

Later, he found that Lippincott had paid Gilliland, now Edison's business manager, an additional $250,000 for the right to sell the machines. Gilliland paid one-third of this amount to Edison's lawyer, John Tomlinson. The selling rights were worth perhaps $50,000. The other $200,000 was a concealed bribe, in return for which Gilliland and Tomlinson had persuaded Edison to sell the patent rights for half their true value.

By the time Edison found out, the conspirators had left the United States for Europe. Lippincott failed to make a success of the business and was soon paralyzed by a stroke. Edison was owed so much for machines that he was able to take over the company, thus regaining control of his patents.

He developed the business slowly but successfully. At first, he thought his two-machine cylinders would be mainly used for office dictation. But the Victor and Columbia companies showed that there was now a huge market for two- and four-minute entertainment discs made for the Victor talking machine, or gramophone, invented by Emile Berliner. So Edison too recorded popular music on cylinders. Later, he also switched to discs.

Making Movies

Meanwhile Edison had also been attracted by the idea of motion pictures. "In the year 1887," he later explained, "the idea occurred to me that it was possible to devise an instrument which should do for the eye what the phonograph does for the ear."

It was well known that the image of an object seen by the eye persisted in the brain for up to a tenth of a second after the object itself was no longer in sight. So a series of still photographs, showing successive positions of a body in

Edison's first movie viewing device, the Kinetoscope, was invented in 1886. In this early version, the clockwork turned a shaft, causing the small pictures to seem to move when viewed through the magnifying eyepiece.

motion, would give an appearance of movement if they could be shown in rapid succession.

Ordinary cameras then used glass plates, which were far too big and clumsy. After a number of failures, Edison found that tiny pictures could be photographed spirally on a celluloid film wrapped around a phonograph-type cylinder. As it turned, sparks from an **induction coil** lit them up one by one. Viewed through a magnifying glass, they gave the illusion of motion. An early effort showed an assistant in a white sheet, waving his arms about.

The breakthrough came when George Eastman, the inventor of the Kodak camera, created continuous strips of celluloid film that could be run through a camera. "Allowing 46 exposures per second, as we did at first," said Edison, "we had to face the fact that the film had to be stopped and started again after each exposure. Now, allowing 1/100 part of a second for every impression that was registered, you can see that almost half of our time was gone, and in the remainder of the time we had to move the film forward the necessary distance for the next exposures.... All this had to be done with the exactness of a watch movement."

Edison's movie camera, which he called a Kinetograph, was a big success. So was the Kinetoscope, a coin-in-the-slot peep-hole machine for showing his films. It had a magnifying glass and a revolving shutter with a hole in it. This revealed the pictures one at a time in rapid succession. Kinetoscope parlors blossomed all over America.

Edison made films for them in the "Black Maria," a 50-foot, black-lined studio with a retractable roof. It could be swung around on a pivot to catch the sun at any time of the day. Boxers, dancers, jugglers, and performing bears appeared in films that lasted up to a minute.

To learn more about Edison's Kinetoscope, scan here:

Thomas Edison and George Eastman (1854–1932) pose with a motion picture camera, 1925.

If Edison had put all his energies into motion pictures, he might well have won a world monopoly. But he was busy with too many other things. He did not patent the Kinetograph and Kinetoscope until 1891, two years after inventing them. Even then, he did not take out European patents because, he said, they weren't worth the $150 fee! He was also slow to develop a system of projecting films on to a screen.

The result was inevitable. Edison made steadily more elaborate films, culminating in thousands of fourteen-minute dramas and comedies. He built a $100,000 studio in the Bronx district of New York. His manufacturing companies reaped huge profits from making equipment. Yet it was only a partial success. His delays had allowed rivals to catch up with him. European manufacturers freely copied his unpatented inventions, developed them, and sold the rights in the United States. Edison once more became involved in a tangle of patent lawsuits that

A frame-by-frame print of the Kinetoscope recording of a sneeze by one of Edison's assistants, Fred Ott. This was the first motion picture ever copyrighted, in 1894.

took sixteen years to resolve. To save further trouble, all the parties involved then poole their patents. Edison's share of the royalties amounted to $1 million a year.

The pool infringed against U.S. laws that prohibited such arrangements. In 1917, it was broken up. By then, Edison was a national legend, wealthy, and loaded with honors. Though devoted to his second wife, Mina, he had no interests outside his work. Henry Ford was one of his few intimate friends.

Final Years

During the First World War, Edison became head of a board of technologists formed to advise on military inventions. He himself thought up several devices for fighting the submarine menace. He set up factories for making benzol, carbolic acid and other chemicals in short supply, and made yet another fortune.

In his later years, he was stocky, but still healthy and active. His hair was white and untidy, his face impassive under bushy eyebrows. But his judgment steadily worsened. He refused to have anything to do with radio receivers for the popular market. He thought they had no future. He changed his mind in 1928, but the Great Depression that began the next year soon cut the demand for radios. In 1931, production was stopped after the Edison companies lost $3 million. A year before, they had stopped making phonographs and records. Edison had stubbornly refused to keep up with improved methods of sound reproduction.

He spent years trying to find a cheap rubber substitute that could be grown in the United States. By 1929, after investigating some 15,000 plants, he had devised a scheme for extracting liquid rubber from goldenrod. But this process was more expensive than imported rubber. Moreover, synthetic rubber had already been invented in Germany.

Edison was almost eighty when he resigned from his companies. His sons by his first wife both proved a disappointment. Thomas Jr. became involved in shady business ventures and committed suicide in 1936. William Leslie, after serving in the American army, eventually became a gentleman farmer and died in 1941.

His sons by Mina, however, were all he could have wished for. Charles became the highly successful head of the Edison business interests. Theodore became

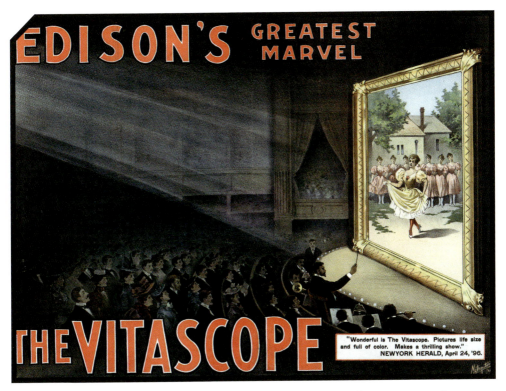

The Vitascope was an early motion picture projector. This advertisement is from 1896.

technical director of the Edison Laboratory, but eventually left to set up as a scientific consultant on his own.

In 1929, Henry Ford arranged a celebration at Dearborn, Michigan, for the fiftieth anniversary of Edison's inventing the electric lamp. Ford shipped in all the surviving equipment from Menlo Park and built a replica of Edison's laboratory. President Herbert Hoover and Madame Marie Curie headed a swarm of notables who came from all over the world to pay homage to Edison. As Hoover was finishing his speech, Edison collapsed.

Doctors quickly revived Edison, but a number of illnesses had taken hold of his ageing frame. He had gastric ulcers, kidney disease, and diabetes. He gradually gave up his laboratory work, spending his days sleeping or reading in the

Edison (center, holding newspaper) speaks with newly elected U.S. President Warren G. Harding during a 1921 camping trip in Maryland. With them are Edison's close friend Henry Ford (left) and industrialist Harvey Firestone (right). Ford (1863–1947) had once worked for Edison, but left to establish an automobile manufacturing empire in Detroit, based on principles of mass production. Firestone (1868–1938) founded the Firestone Rubber Company, one of the first manufacturers of automobile tires, in 1900. Harding (1865–1923) was a popular president, but scandals that emerged after his death in office ruined his reputation.

garden of his West Orange home. He would allow only Mina to take care of him. He insisted on measuring out his own medicine and on studying his own blood tests through a microscope on his bed. On October 17, 1931, he fell into a coma. The next day, he died at the age of eighty-four.

Man and Myth

During his lifetime, Edison was a legend, praised by the leading scientists of the day. He was responsible for major inventions—among them the development of the multiplex telegraph, the microphone, the phonograph, electric lighting, and motion pictures—as well as numerous smaller inventions. But the second half of Edison's life was something of an **anticlimax**. Many of his large business interests never wholly fulfilled their promise. He was continually plagued with lawsuits over patent rights. He did not follow through his successes, and he had several costly business failures.

This was all the more surprising as he had always been not only enterprising, but commercial. Edison did not try to invent useless or impossible gadgets. Indeed, he was scarcely an original inventor at all. Throughout his life he kept abreast of developments in a dozen different fields, and often built on these to invent devices that would be of use to large numbers of people. He had gone into manufacturing only because industrialists did not always share his vision. He could not bear to see a useful invention lying idle. Making inventions profitable was his main goal in life.

Edison did everything on a vast scale, so it is not surprising that he became a multimillionaire. He could have retired at thirty. Instead, he preferred to keep on working until he was almost eighty.

Money itself meant little to him. He used it to finance the work that interested him. As a telegraphist, he had plunged his wages on the best experimental equipment he could afford. When he became rich, he invested millions of dollars in his projects. Setbacks rarely upset him. When he was sixty-seven years old, seven of Edison's factories burned down. As they were **underinsured**, he lost something like a million dollars. Within thirty-six hours, he had 1,500 men rebuilding even bigger factories under his personal supervision. "No one's ever too old to make a fresh start," he said.

Edison never lost the common touch, nor his gift for inspiring those who worked for him. He was a brilliant storyteller. He was also a compulsive practical joker. He carried on chewing tobacco and spitting the juice on the floor, even when he was a multimillionaire. When he had a problem to solve, he worked day and night with only brief snatches of sleep for days on end. His "muckers," as he called his favorite workmen, never refused to work with him.

Edison paid good but not exceptional wages. He had no sympathy for trade unions. Eighty men whom he had trained to make light bulbs threatened to strike if he fired an unsatisfactory workman. Edison needed them. So he kept the man on. But he secretly invented machinery for making the bulbs. When it was ready, he fired the workman. His colleagues, as promised, went out on strike. "They have been out ever since," he said grimly.

Edison was ill at ease in the world of high finance. He looked on money as a means, and could never understand men who regarded it as an end. He was overly trusting. He was outmaneuvered repeatedly by such financial geniuses as Jay Gould and J. P. Morgan. He was swindled by several individuals, often for huge sums.

Edison was a good judge of men in the sense that he repeatedly built up teams who successfully carried through his projects. He seemed little interested in people at a deeper level. He had numerous acquaintances but few real friends. One of the few exceptions was Henry Ford, the automobile manufacturer.

His flair for publicity was exceptional. He cultivated reporters and gave them sensational stories about his inventions, often before he had perfected them. He had a collection of **anecdotes** about himself that became steadily more colorful over the years. He delighted in sitting for the camera. He had studio portraits taken regularly and was always eager to pose for press photographers against a background of impressive equipment, peering intently into a test tube.

He "got away with it" because he always fulfilled his promises, at least in his early years. His countrymen liked him too because he was a prime example of the American dream, a poor country boy who made good. He was plainspoken, unassuming, eager to poke fun at intellectuals, and always ready—even when rich—to pitch in with his men, covering himself with grease, when necessary, and even snatching sleep on a bench.

Yet he never curried favor with his friends, his business associates, or the American public. He caused a furor by announcing that he did not believe in a personal God, only a "Supreme Intelligence." But he admitted the possibility of survival after death. He repeatedly attacked mindless fact learning and preferred teaching through play because it made learning a pleasure. He was an early opponent of capital punishment. "There are wonderful possibilities in each human soul," he said. "I cannot endorse a method of punishment which destroys the last chance of usefulness."

Edison had his faults. He was sometimes insensitive to other people's feelings. His practical jokes were often far from funny. His passion for work led him to neglect his own children, especially those by his first wife. When driven into a corner, as in the argument over the relative merits of alternating current and direct current, he could hit below the belt.

Was Thomas Alva Edison a genius? He once defined genius as "one percent inspiration and ninety-nine percent perspiration." By that standard, he clearly qualified. If Edison had invented only the electric light bulb, he would have been noteworthy. That he also gave the world the microphone, the Kinetoscope, the phonograph, and scores of other devices makes him one of the greatest inventors the world has ever known. Most important, Edison pioneered the industrial research laboratory, thus making possible the technological progress of the twentieth and twenty-first centuries.

 TEXT-DEPENDENT QUESTIONS

1. Who invented the Victor talking machine?
2. What was Edison's first movie camera called?
3. What industrialist was Edison's good friend?

 RESEARCH PROJECT

Using your school library or the internet, find out more about William Kennedy-Laurie Dickson, one of Edison's "muckers," who had an important role in the early motion picture industry. Write a two-page report about his life and accomplishments and share it with your class.

Chronology

1847

Thomas Alva Edison is born in Milan, Ohio, on February 11.

1854

Edison family moves to Port Huron, Michigan.

1859

Becomes "candy butcher" on the Detroit train.

1861

The American Civil War begins, lasting until 1865.

1863

Edison begins work as a telegraph operator.

1868

Applies for his first patent, for a vote-recording machine.

1869

Resigns from Western Union in Boston to become a full-time inventor. Applies for patent on stock ticker. Moves to New York, and joins the Gold Indicator Company. Leaves to set up as an "electrical engineer." Marries his first wife, Mary.

1870

Western Union purchases his stock ticker.

1871

Sets up as a manufacturer of stock tickers.

1872

Applies for patent on automatic telegraph.

1873
First of several visits to England.

1874
The multiplex telegraph perfected.

1875
The motograph circumvents patents for the Page relay.

1876
Swindled by financier Jay Gould.

1877
Builds Menlo Park research laboratory. Perfects telephone transmitter (microphone). Applies for patent on phonograph.

1878
Applies for patent on first electric lamp. Edison Electric Light Company is established.

1879
Applies for patent on vacuum lamp with platinum filament. Applies for patent on carbon filament lamp.

1880
Applies for patent on new method of extracting ore. Lighting plant installed in S.S. *Columbia*. First run of electric train at Menlo Park. Edison Electric Illuminating Company of New York is formed.

1880
Sets up his own manufacturing companies.

1881
Moves his headquarters to New York. Pearl Street site bought for New York central station.

1882
Lights switched on in New York.

1884
Death of Mary, his first wife.

1886
Marries his second wife, Mina.

1887
Builds new laboratory in West Orange, New Jersey.

1888
Improved phonograph perfected. His manufacturing companies merge with Edison Electric to form the Edison General Electric Company.

1889
The Kinetograph and Kinetoscope invented.

1890
Ore-crushing plant opens in Ogdensburg, New Jersey.

1891
Edison General Electric is merged with Thomson–Houston to form the General Electric Company. Edison is ousted. Applies for patents for the Kinetograph and Kinetoscope.

1908
Motion Picture Patents Corporation formed as patent pool.

1909
Nickel-iron-alkaline storage battery perfected.

1911
Edison's own companies combined in Thomas A. Edison Inc.

1914
First World War begins. Fire destroys seven of Edison's factories in West Orange.

1915
Serves as president of the Navy Consulting Board for inventions.

1916
Begins work on anti-submarine devices.

1917
The United States enters the war.

1918
The First World War ends on November 11.

1922
Nominated as "greatest living American" in a *New York Times* poll.

1927
Develops a natural substitute for rubber.

1928
Awarded Congressional Medal of Honor.

1929
Suffers from severe illnesses, including diabetes and kidney disease.

1931
Dies on October 18.

Further Reading

Barnham, Kay. *Thomas Edison*. Chicago: Raintree, 2014.

Cawthorne, Nigel. *Tesla vs. Edison: The Life-Long Feud that Electrified the World*. New York: Chartwell Books, 2016.

DeGraaf, Leonard. *Edison and the Rise of Innovation*. New York: Sterling Signature, 2013.

Freeberg, Ernest. *The Age of Edison: Electric Light and the Invention of Modern America*. New York: Penguin Books, 2013.

Jonnes, Jill. *Empires of Light: Edison, Tesla, Westinghouse, and the Race to Electrify the World*. New York: Random House, 2003.

Martin, Joel, and William J. Birnes. *Edison vs. Tesla: The Battle over Their Last Invention*. New York: Skyhorse Publishing, 2017.

Morus, Iwan Rhys. *The Oxford Illustrated History of Science*. New York: Oxford University Press, 2017.

Stross, Randall. *The Wizard of Menlo Park: How Thomas Alva Edison Invented the Modern World*. New York: Three Rivers Press, 2008.

Wootton, David. *The Invention of Science: A New History of the Scientific Revolution*. New York: Harper Perennial, 2016.

Internet Resources

https://www.nps.gov/edis/index.htm

Website of Thomas Edison National Historical Park in West Orange, New Jersey, which preserves Edison's home and research laboratory. The site includes information on Edison and his inventions, historic photographs, and other information.

http://www.menloparkmuseum.org

The purpose of the Thomas Edison Center at Menlo Park is to educate the public about Edison, his significant accomplishments at Menlo Park, and his impact on modern research and development.

http://edison.rutgers.edu

Since 1978 the Rutgers University School of Arts and Sciences has been editing the five million pages of documents that chronicle the extraordinary life and achievements of Thomas Alva Edison. Visitors to this site can explore Edison's documents, read essays about his innovations, and view videos that demonstrate the technologies he developed.

http://www.pbs.org/wgbh/nova

The website of NOVA, a science series that airs on PBS. The series produces in-depth science programming on a variety of topics, from the latest breakthroughs in technology to the deepest mysteries of the natural world.

http://www.livescience.com

The website Live Science is regularly updated with articles on scientific topics and new developments or discoveries.

Series Glossary of Key Terms

anomaly—something that differs from the expectations generated by an established scientific idea. Anomalous observations may inspire scientists to reconsider, modify, or come up with alternatives to an accepted theory or hypothesis.

evidence—test results and/or observations that may either help support or help refute a scientific idea. In general, raw data are considered evidence only once they have been interpreted in a way that reflects on the accuracy of a scientific idea.

experiment—a scientific test that involves manipulating some factor or factors in a system in order to see how those changes affect the outcome or behavior of the system.

hypothesis—a proposed explanation for a fairly narrow set of phenomena, usually based on prior experience, scientific background knowledge, preliminary observations, and logic.

natural world—all the components of the physical universe, as well as the natural forces at work on those things.

objective—to consider and represent facts without being influenced by biases, opinions, or emotions. Scientists strive to be objective, not subjective, in their reasoning about scientific issues.

observe—to note, record, or attend to a result, occurrence, or phenomenon.

science—knowledge of the natural world, as well as the process through which that knowledge is built through testing ideas with evidence gathered from the natural world.

subjective—referring to something that is influenced by biases, opinions, and/or emotions. Scientists strive to be objective, not subjective, in their reasoning about scientific issues.

test—an observation or experiment that could provide evidence regarding the accuracy of a scientific idea. Testing involves figuring out what one would expect to observe if an idea were correct and comparing that expectation to what one actually observes.

theory—a broad, natural explanation for a wide range of phenomena in science. Theories are concise, coherent, systematic, predictive, and broadly applicable, often integrating and generalizing many hypotheses. Theories accepted by the scientific community are generally strongly supported by many different lines of evidence. However, theories may be modified or overturned as new evidence is discovered.

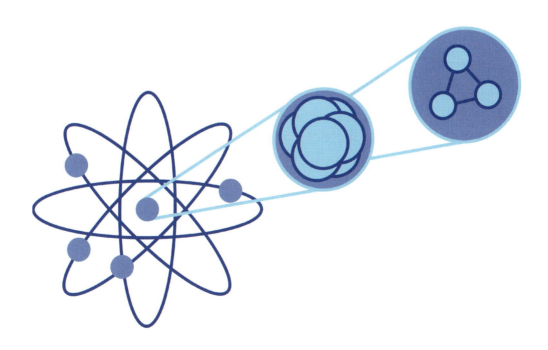

Index

A

AC (alternating current), 58, 64 (QR code), 65, 66, 83
Adams, Milton, 18
air pump, 33
alternating current (AC), 58, 64 (QR code), 65, 66, 83
America (1847), 7
American Civil War, 11, 21, 70
American Speaking Telephone Company, 38
anecdote, 68, 82
antenna, 64
anticlimax, 68, 81
Appalachian mines, 65
arc light, 44, 45, 46
Ashley, J.W., 22
Atlantic Telegraph Company, 29
automatic telegraph, 27, 28
Automatic Telegraph Company, 27, 28, 29

B

bamboo, 53, 54
Barker, George, 45
Batchelor, Charles, 51, 70–71
battery, 64
Battle of Shiloh (1862), 11, 12, 13, 69
Bell receiver, 38
Bell system, 38
Bell, Alexander Graham, 35, 36–37, 51, 72, 73
belt drive, 50
Berliner, Emile, 73
Bethlehem Steel Company, 65
Biography Company, 70
Black Maria (studio), 75
Boston (Massachusetts), 14
branch line, 46
British Post Office, 28
Brown, Charles, 70–71

C

camera, 70, 74
candy butcher, 10, 11, 69
Cape Horn, 54
capitalists, 18
carbon, 50, 51
carbon button telephone, 45
cardboard filament, 52
celluloid film, 74, 75
central power station, 46, 55, 56, 59
circuit, 32, 38, 46
Coffin, Charles A., 60
Coffin, Morgan, 60
Congress (United States), 18
copper, 52
cotton filament, 51–52
crank, 32, 40
Culture (Francis R. Upton), 34, 50
Curie, Marie (Madame), 79
cylinder, 42, 72

D

dash, 13, 15, 39
Davy, Humphry (Sir), 45
DC (direct current), 58, 65, 83
Decline and Fall of the Roman Empire (Gibbon), 10
Detroit (Michigan), 10, 11, 12
Detroit Free Press (newspaper), 11–12, 69
diaphragm, 32, 35
Dickens, 10
Dickson, William Kennedy-Laurie, 70–71
Dictionary of Sciences, 10
direct current (DC), 58, 65, 83
dot, 13, 15, 39
drill, 33
duplex, 6, 17, 18, 28
dynamo, 44, 45, 50, 53, 54, 55

E

Eastman, George, 75, 76
Eckert, T.T. (General), 29
economic depression, 28
Edison and Unger, 25, 28
Edison Electric Light Company, 46, 49, 51, 52, 54–55, 59, 60
Edison Electric Lighting Station, 44, 53
Edison General Electric Company, 60
Edison Illuminating Company of New York, 55, 59
Edison laboratory, 79
Edison Lamp Company, 55
Edison Machine Works, 55

Edison Village, 34
Edison, Charles (son), 63, 78
Edison, Madeleine (daughter), 63
Edison, Marion (daughter), 26, 62
Edison, Mina Miller (second wife), 62, 63, 78, 80
Edison, Nancy Elliot (mother), 7, 9, 10 (QR code), 26
Edison, Samuel Ogden (father), 7, 9, 10, 26, 33
Edison, Theodore (son), 63, 78–79
Edison, Thomas, 10, 18, 22, 27, 30, 33, 37, 39, 41, 45, 46, 51, 53, 62, 75
    as an entrepreneur, 11–12, 59–60, 69
    as an inventor, 10, 13, 16–18, 23, 34, 36, 80–81
    appearance of, 15, 17, 25, 45
    birth, childhood, death, 7, 8, 9, 11, 13, 20, 24, 63, 78, 80
    electricity, interest in, 10, 60–61
    electrictelegraph, 13, 14, 16
    faults, 83
    health, 37, 78, 79–80
    incandescent light, 44, 46, 47, 49 (QR code), 52, 54, 81–82
    as a manufacturer, 25, 72
    portraits of, 20, 32, 35, 40, 58, 68, 76
    as a prankster, 14, 16, 42, 65
    with the press, 82
    quotes, 10, 18, 22, 27, 30, 33, 37, 39, 41, 45, 46, 51, 53, 62, 75
    research, passion for, 69, 83
    resourcefulness, 21, 37, 81
Edison, Thomas Junior (son), 26, 62, 78
Edison, William Leslie (son), 62, 78
electric chair, 65
electric current, 13
electric light, 35, 45–46, 48, 55, 56, 60–61, 70–71
electric locomotive, 64
electric motor, 72
electric pen, 28
electric telegraph, 13
electrical engineering, 22
electrical resistance, 50
electricity, 45, 46, 55, 56
electricity-generating plants, 59
electromagnet, 6, 13, 22
electromagnetic induction, 35

electronic lamp, 64, 65
emboss, 20, 22
Embossing Translating Telegraph, 38

F
Faraday, Michael, 45
feeder and main system, 53
filament, 50, 51, 53, 63
filibuster, 6, 18
First World War, 78
Ford, Henry, 65, 78, 79, 82
frock coat, 20, 25
fuse, 44, 46, 52

G
gas engine, 65
gas light, 55, 57
General Electric Company, 60
generating plant, 46
generator, 52
genius, 83
Gilliland, Ezra, 62, 73
Glenmont, 63
Gold Indicator Company, 21, 22
golden rod, 78
Gould, Jay, 27, 29, 30, 82
Gourand, George, 70–71
gramophone, 39
gramophone (Victor talking machine), 73
Grand Trunk Herald (newspaper), 12
Grand Trunk Railroad, 10, 11, 12
graphophone, 72
Gray, Elisha, 35
Great Depression, 78

H
Harrington, George, 27, 29
Havana, Cuba, 54
Hayes, Rutherford B. (US President), 42
Hoover, Herbert (President), 79
Huron canal, 7

I
incandescent light, 44, 46, 47, 49 (QR code), 52, 54, 81–82
induction coil, 68, 74
insulation, 54

iron disc, 35, 38, 39
iron ore crushing, 65, 67, 71
ironworks, 65

J
Japan, 54
Johnson, Edward H., 27, 34

K
Kinetograph, 75, 76
Kinetoscope, 70–71, 74, 75 (QR code), 76, 77, 83
Kinetoscope parlor, 75
Kodak camera, 75
Kruesi, John, 39

L
lamp, 53, 54
lamp post, 55
lathe, 33
Latimer, Lewis, 51
Laws, Samuel S. (Doctor), 18, 21–22
Lefferts, Marshall (General), 22, 23, 24, 25
light bulb, 47, 48, 49 (QR code), 50, 55, 57, 60
light engineering industry, 17
Lippincott, Jesse W., 73
Little, George D., 27
low-powered electric light, 46
Lowrey, Grosvenor, 46

M
Mackenzie, J.U., 14
magnifying glass, 74, 75
main line, 46
mains, 44, 52
Marconi, Guglielmo, 64
Medal of Honor (Union Army), 70
Memphis (Tennessee), 14, 17
Menlo Park (New York City), 33–34, 35, 38, 42, 49, 52–53, 69, 79
Michigan (US), 9
microphone, 32, 38, 41, 64, 83
microscope, 33
Milan (Ohio), 7
mill machine, 33
mimeograph, 20, 28
Moore, William H., 54
Morgan, J.Pierpont, 49, 60, 61, 82

Morse code, 6, 13, 14, 15, 24, 39, 62
Morse, Samuel F.B., 14
motion pictures, 73–74, 76
motor car, 64, 65
Mount Clemens (Michigan), 13
muckers, 70, 71
Murray, Joseph T., 27

N
New York City Hall, 56
New York lighting system, 59
Niagara Falls, 65
nickel, 49

O
octuplex telegraph, 30
odorscope, 34
Ontario (Canada), 7
Ott, Fred, 70, 71, 77
Ott, John, 25, 70–71

P
Pacific Telegraph Company, 29
Panama Canal, 54
parallel (light), 46
patent
    definition of, 6
    rights, 29, 35, 71, 76, 78
    specific to Edison, 17, 19, 24, 26–28, 36, 41, 46
Patent Office, 33
Pearl Street, 53, 59
phonograph, 35, 38, 39, 40, 41, 42 (QR code), 50, 70–71, 72–73, 78, 83
pirate, 32, 39
platinum fliament, 46, 48, 49, 50
Pope, Frank, 21, 22, 23
Port Huron (Michigan), 10, 11, 12, 14, 33
Prescott, George, 28
Principles (Newton), 11
punch, 33

Q
quadruplex telegraph, 28, 29

R
radio, 58, 64, 78
recording diaphragm, 40

records, 78
Reiff, Josiah, 27
research, 69, 83
resistance, 32, 37
Robber Barons, 29
Rocky Mountains (Canada), 45
royalty, 32, 42
rubber, 78

S
S.S. *Columbia* (ship), 54
Sawyer, William E., 52
scarlet fever, 9, 13, 37
series (light), 46
Shakespeare, 10
shares, 60
soot, 50
Sprengel pump, 49
steam, 50, 54, 55
steam engine, 55, 64
Stilwell, Mary (wife), 26, 61
stock ticker, 18–19, 23, 25, 28
Stratford Junction (rail station), 16
stylus, 39, 40, 72
submarine, 64–65, 78
synthetic rubber, 78

T
T.A. Edison Construction Department, 59
tar, 50
tasimeter, 34
technological progress, 64
telegraph, 6, 11, 14, 15, 34
telegraph operator, 14, 16
telegraph relay, 20, 28
Telegrapher, 22
telegraphy, 14, 21, 22 (QR code), 34, 41, 64
telephone, 35, 36, 38, 41, 45
Tesla, Nicola, 64 (QR code)

Thomson-Houston, 60
Tomlinson, John, 73
transformer, 32, 37
transmitter, 36, 38, 39
tripod-mounted megaphone, 34
two-machine cylinder, 73
typhoid fever, 58, 61

U
U.S. Department of the Treasury, 27
underinsured, 68, 81
Union Army, 70
Upton, Francis R. (aka Culture), 34, 50

V
Victor talking machine (gramophone), 73
Vienna (tavern), 7
Villard, Henry, 54
voltage, 44, 50, 65
voltmeter, 44, 56
von Hemholtz, Hermann, 34
vote recorder, 17, 18

W
Wall street (NYC), 55
Wangemann, Theo, 70–71
"War of the Currents," 66
Wardst factory (Newark), 25
West Orange laboratory, 61, 63, 68, 72, 92
Western Union, 16–18, 22, 24–25, 27–28, 30, 38
Westinghouse Electrical and Manufacturing
    Company, 65
Westinghouse, George, 65, 66
widower, 58, 62
Williams, Charles Jr., 18

Y
yellow fever, 54

About the Author

Karen Ellis was educated at St. John's University in New York, where she graduated with a degree in history. She has traveled widely in the United States, as well as in the Middle East, Malaysia, Australia, and Canada. She has written many newspaper and magazine articles. This is her first book.

Photo Credits

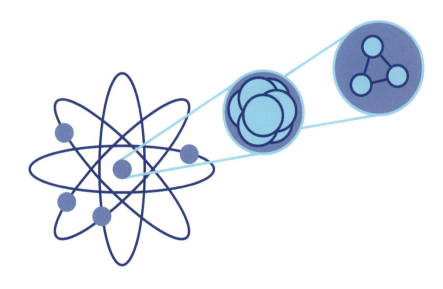